LINDEMANN GROUP

Peter Schiessl

AF807908

CorelDRAW 2017

&

CorelDRAW Home and Student X8

Training Book

WITH MANY EXERCISES

Something looks different?
Use Window-Workspace-Default

Lindemann Group
PETER SCHIESSL

CorelDRAW 2017

&

CorelDraw Home and Student X8

TRAINING BOOK WITH MANY EXERCISES

ISBN 978-1-973163-45-9
Print on Demand since October, 10th 2017
Lindemann Group

Fortnerstr. 8, 80933 Munich, Germany
post@kamiprint.de
www.kamiprint.de
www.lindemann-beer.com

Table of Contents

Chapter 1

1. Principles

In this book, we systematically describe CorelDRAW from the beginning and with many exercises. But to use this book and the powerful CorelDRAW program, you must have some prerequisites.

1.1 Your Prerequisites

CorelDRAW will be described from beginning, but not general computer and Windows basics:

- Experience drawing with mouse and keyboard.
- Windows basics: how to save files, open, rename, and copy files to a USB stick or to another folder.
- Modifying your Windows system by installing a printer, setting up a printer (e.g. print quality, print darkness, paper type) or changing the resolution of your monitor shouldn't be a problem for you.

These prerequisites are a sample of computer basics knowledge you should know well. If not, a computer basic training is recommended before you start with computer graphics.

That way, you will avoid frustrations and have much more fun with computers and this computer graphic course.

1.2 CorelDRAW or Photo-Paint

Why CorelDRAW, why Corel Photo-Paint? In practice, most times both programs are useful because they complete each other.

- Photo-Paint is for working with photos. Photos on the computer are so-called pixel-pictures because, simply, photos are created dot by dot, and the color of each dot is saved.
- CorelDRAW is used to make graphic works with prepared photos, text and clipart's such as presentation charts, promotion sheets or business cards/logos.

This working separation results from the big difference between both programs, similar to the difference between photos and drawings. This be explained further in this workbook.

1.3 Setup and Workspace

- If you have a Corel-DVD the installation starts automatically when you insert it.
  - ↳ Or you can download and install from www.corel.com and use the program for 15 days free.
- To change or delete the CorelDraw program with Windows 10, click the Windows symbol in the bottom left corner of your screen, then settings, then Apps & Features. In this window click on the CorelDRAW symbol and select first Delete, then you can choose Delete or Modify.

When starting for the first time, a Welcome Screen appears with a short introduction into CorelDRAW and there you can choose the workspace:

Looks different? Use Window-Workspace-Default

- Lite is more reduced with as few symbols as possible, making it an easy introduction to CorelDRAW.
- Default is the usual workspace for users with experience in CorelDRAW or other graphic software.
- Touch is suitable for tablets and touch-enabled devices.

> We use the "Default" workspace in the following pages, but you can change your workspace layout anytime between the Lite workspace and the default when necessary.

1.4 The Corel-Family (Samples)

The download is part of a package. Here a short presentation of the parts of this package.

The main content of CorelDRAW Suite:

- CorelDRAW is the vector-based program for graphics, design work, posters, presentations, business cards and more.
  - ↳ Most functions of Corel PHOTO-PAINT for photos are integrated into CorelDRAW so the switch to PHOTO-PAINT is mostly not necessary.
- Corel PHOTO-PAINT is for working with photos. Photos in the computer are created by scanning or taking with a digital photo camera, which are saved point for point (pixel = picture elements).
  - ↳ So, you can't click on an element and mark it because there are no elements (objects, e.g. a ball, airplane, people…) in a digital photo, there are only points with different colors.

After the installation, you'll find in your start menu, and possibly on your desktop, these symbols:

- CorelDRAW: the drawing program
- Corel Photo-Paint: the photo program
- Corel Connect: with an internet connection, you can download and insert into your projects photos, clipart's, backgrounds, frames, fonts, etc.
- Duplexing Wizard: helps by printing on the front and back of the paper.

More Add-Ins:

Using the "Launch" symbol, you can start installed apps and plug-ins or download more additional apps and plug-ins. Please take a look at the available apps, plug-ins and extensions by clicking "Get More...." because this content changes sometimes.

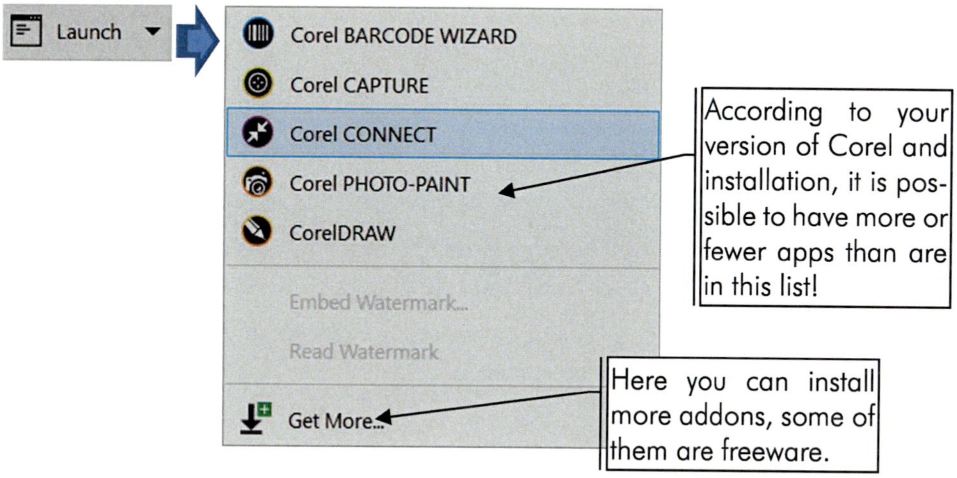

- With the "Corel BARCODE WIZARD" you can make barcodes (EAN, ISBN ....) yourself or modify existing barcodes.

You can start the main Corel programs by clicking start/programs/CorelDRAW. Additional apps and plug-ins you can start in CorelDRAW with the "Launch" symbol.

1.4.1 The Fonts

- In Corel Connect (Content Exchange/Fonts) you'll find many more fonts and can install them by clicking the right mouse button on a font you want to install.
  - ➯ Here you can find many fonts with foreign special letters e.g. Chinese or Korean and many symbol fonts.
  - ➯ By the Home and Student Suite the font list is reduced and you find only some sample fonts.
- There are more fonts you can find on the internet as freeware, or you can buy them from many shops, e.g. MyFonts.com or www.linotype.com – the classic font source for publishers and designers.

> Don't install too many fonts you don't use because every installed font consumes internal PC memory.

1.5 The ClipArt

A large amount of ClipArt can be found by clicking Connect/Clipart:

- You can drag a picture with the left mouse button in the CorelDRAW drawing (drag and drop) or insert a picture with the right mouse button, a preview appears if you hold mouse some seconds over icon.
- You can use the windows explorer and connect for other folders with pictures or clipart, too. Only choose the folder for the content you want to view.

1.6 Preliminary Considerations

Think first with paper before turning on the PC!

1.6.1 The Customers

A good cook cooks to the taste of his customers. Similarly, to decide if your graphic work is good, you must consider if it matches your customers' needs. So, think first about your target group.

Some suggestions:

- Advertisement for a music festival or business company?
- Birthday party for child turning 4 or 14 years old, or for a company event?

Generally, you can say that a younger customer enjoys more colorful and crazier designs.

Think about the quality requirements for the printed end product.

- The print quality must be very different between an invitation for a private birthday and a pamphlet for a tourist agency.
  - ↳ Your home printer can be good enough to start, but you may need to print with a professional printing company!

The print quality of the end product is very important and must be considered when starting your project. For example, with professional printing you need photos in high resolution. Today, many people have very good color laser printers, but they are not good enough for a professional advertisement. Additionally, if you print in a print shop, the professional there can take a last look at your work and help you get that perfect finish for your graphic work.

> Compare your work with those of the professionals. These lessons are free in print shop, because the best paid graphic professionals sit in the advertising departments.

1.6.2 First Drafts

First blueprints and preliminary considerations are mostly done faster and better on paper.

Then you have to think if the graphic program CorelDRAW or the photo program Corel PHOTO-PAINT is better for the job, or if you need both – for most projects you will need Photo-Paint to prepare the photos and CorelDRAW to combine the photos with text and graphic elements.

> Save your work early and make backups regularly on external media or on the cloud so you don't lose your work and good ideas.

Chapter 2

2. Vector or Pixel?

CorelDRAW is a vector drawing program, while Corel PHOTO-PAINT stores the images as pixel graphics.

2.1 Vector-Graphics

With vector graphics, drawn elements (lines, circles, rectangles ...) are stored as mathematic functions (vectors): Line from point x1, y1 to x2, y2 with line width and line color.

For a line, therefore, the coordinate of the start and end point is noted, in addition to the line thickness, color and type.

- For this reason, each drawn element can be subsequently resized or moved.
- Even with an enormous magnification, the lines always remain sharp.

In addition to CorelDRAW, there are numerous other vector-oriented programs, and therefore some different file extensions are used.

> Of course, all CAD programs are also vector programs (CAD = computer-aided design = computer-aided drawing, programs for technical drawing).

2.2 Pixel-Photos

Similar to the screen, a picture is composed of many points. The color is stored for each of these dots (or pixels). Your screen might display the image with 1920 horizontal and 1080 vertical points (= Full HD resolution) - depending on the settings of your monitor.

This explains why image files become quite large and the following problem arises:

> small file - poor image quality
> or
> good picture quality - large file.

If pixel images of poor quality are increased, the dots are clearly visible. Instead of straight lines, stairs are recognizable as on old dot matrix printers.

Overview pixel-graphics

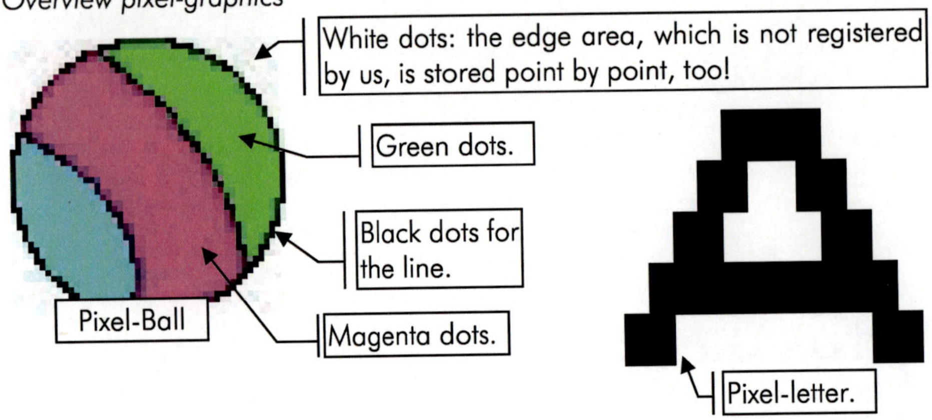

Compressing (Simplified explanation):

- When photos have large areas with small color differences, such as blue skies, high compression is possible:
  - ↳ Here, the compression function can be used to reduce the file size: instead of AAABBBBBCCCC, a formula can store this shorter as "3A5B4C".
  - ↳ In addition, other methods are employed, e.g. a reduction of the details and color differences and dividing into blocks that are 8x8 points each.
- Drawbacks:
  - ↳ Each time you load or save, the computer must calculate the compression.
  - ↳ A low-quality loss arises because the original image is slightly changed. This difference in quality, however, only occurs at higher compression rates above 20:1.

The best compression comes from the .jpg file format, which has therefore become the standard format for photos. In PHOTO-PAINT file-save as and select as jpg as the file type.

jpg

2.3 BY COMPARISON

The differences between the two formats explain the advantages and disadvantages.

Advantages of vector graphics (CorelDRAW):

- Small files with sharp, precise lines and edges.
- Objects (e.g., rectangle, circle) can be changed as desired.
- Special effects are possible, e.g. adding shadow to a text.

For that, still pixel graphics (Photo-Paint)?

- Pixel graphics are an unavoidable evil because a scanner scans line-by-line, dot-by-dot, saving the color of each dot.
  - ↳ Also, a digital camera stores the pixel by dot, e.g. from 18 million points per image.
  - ↳ Thus, all digital photos are pixel images.

- Another application case for a pixel program is painting as with a brush and color on a canvas. Many advertising graphics use this effect e.g. for pseudo-children's pictures.

However, the border CorelDRAW to Corel Photo-Paint runs smoothly. Detailed painting to drawing, e.g. a wintery house with snow on the roof and smoky chimney, is already more useful in CorelDRAW because it can be corrected and changed at any time, and because e.g. a window is drawn only once, then copied as often as required, and Photo-Paint is to correct and prepare photos or copy an object out of a photo to use in a CorelDraw presentation.

2.4 DIVISION OF LABOR IN PRACTICE

- First, prepare the pictures or photos in PHOTO-PAINT:
  - ✎ Scan or edit images (cut out objects, correct brightness, etc.)
- Then, complete the presentation in CorelDRAW:
  - ✎ Load images, add text and custom drawing elements.
- Consider advertising: there are photos (photo-paint) combined with other background and text (CorelDRAW).

For CorelDRAW	For PHOTO-PAINT (Pixel)
Presentations	Scan and edit images (for example, correct brightness, cut away edges).
Leaflets	Edit photos (for example, create an image section).
Title pages	Paint or modify images or clipart in pixel format.
Painting (detailed)	Painting like children.
Drawings	Cut objects from photos (e.g. a person. This object can be inserted into other files or photos).
Business cards etc.	

In PHOTO-PAINT, if possible, do not add text as text is converted into pixel patterns and cannot be changed afterwards. It is better to only edit pure photos in PHOTO-PAINT and add texts only in CorelDRAW.

CorelDRAW is not designed for text processing on a large scale. With a lot of text, work this way: prepare the pictures in Photo-Paint, the graphics elements in CorelDRAW, and import the results to a modern word processing program and assemble with text (layout). If graphics elements are marked in Corel, they can be exported to the .wmf or .emf format, and then they can easily be inserted into all Microsoft programs.

2.5 The File Types

2.5.1 Theory File Endings

There are many different drawing and painting programs. Each of these programs uses a specific file extension. Why?

- The file name can be up to 255 characters from Windows 95 onwards. Even empty keys and customary characters may be used, but no "\" (backslash, because it is used to separate folders).
- The file extension usually consists of three or four letters separated by a dot from the file name.
  - ↳ In addition, a symbol for each data type and an explanatory text, e.g. "Data Type CorelDRAW Graphics" is shown in Windows.
  - ↳ The file extension indicates the program with which a file was created.
- As an illustration:
  - ↳ Filename.cdr (cdr as file extension for CorelDRAW).
  - ↳ Filename.cpt (cpt as file extension for Corel Photo-Paint).

.
*.cdr
*.cpt

2.5.2 Show File Extensions

So, it's handy to see the file extensions. Since Windows 95, the file extensions are unfortunately no longer displayed automatically. A brief guide for Windows 10 on how to do this:

- Start the Windows Explorer, and open the options on the right side of the map view. In the menu that appears choose the map "View", and remove the mark by the option "Hide extensions for known file types"

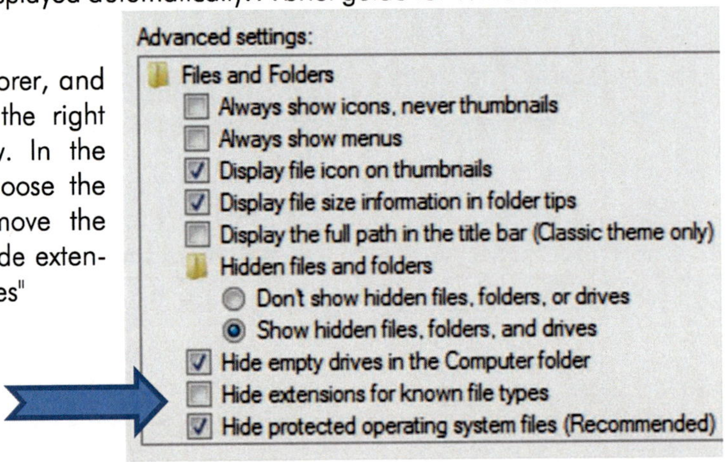

2.5.3 Convert Data Types

Usually, files can only be edited further in the source program. But not with good graphics programs. In Corel, almost every picture or graphics file can be imported.

- ClipArt and vector files should never be opened in PHOTO-PAINT as this means a loss of quality due to the conversion to pixel format.

PHOTO-PAINT only for photos (=Pixel pictures),
CorelDRAW for vector graphics!

2.5.4 Example File Extensions

A certain knowledge of the file endings is useful to recognize the file identities:

File extensions for vector graphics (drawings, graphics)	
cdr	CorelDRAW-drawing.
ai	Adobe Illustrator file
eps	Encapsulated Postscript: standard format for vector graphics (Originally Adobe printer language).
dwg	AutoCAD-drawing (abbreviation of drawing).
wmf	Windows Metafile: a format used by Microsoft, therefore, can be used in MS programs (e.g. Word) as well as emf (enhanced metafile).

The ClipArt elements from the CorelDRAW package are also stored in the cdr format, like the CorelDRAW drawings, and could therefore also be drawn.

File extensions for pixel graphics (photos, painted pictures)	
cpt	Corel Photo-Paint-picture
pcx	Previously, many ClipArt files were stored in this formerly widespread format.
bmp	Bitmap: Windows background images were saved earlier in this format. Today they are rare, since there was no compression!
tif	Target Image File: Formerly standard format for scanned images.
gif	Graphic Image File: Good compression, therefore recommended for pixel graphics, but max. 256 colors, not enough for photos.
png	Portable Network Graphic: With no-loss compression.
pcd	Kodak-Photo-CD-Pictures: Excellent picture quality, accordingly large files. When copying to the hard disk, the desired quality of the image can be reduced accordingly.
jpg	Very good compression, therefore very recommendable, especially for a very large image being copied to the cloud. Meanwhile, it is the standard format for digital photos. Also, most digital cameras save in this format, usually with very high compression.
Jp2	JPEG2000 is the successor of jpg. Compression of jpg has been further improved, and additional information can be stored, e.g. recording date and recording settings, which may be useful for digital photo equipment.
raw	Without compression = without quality loss, used by professional photographers.

On the Internet, the transfer times are the problem, which is why pictures should be as small as possible: use jpg for photos going to the internet, and gif for drawn elements.

2.6 The Window "Hints"

A useful and helpful feature is the "Notes" window is displayed on the right.

There you will find information and instructions on the currently selected tool and you can read more detailed help texts with the hyperlinks shown below.

Use the X symbol to close this window, reopen with "Window/Dockers/Hints".

Now it is time to start our first drawing.

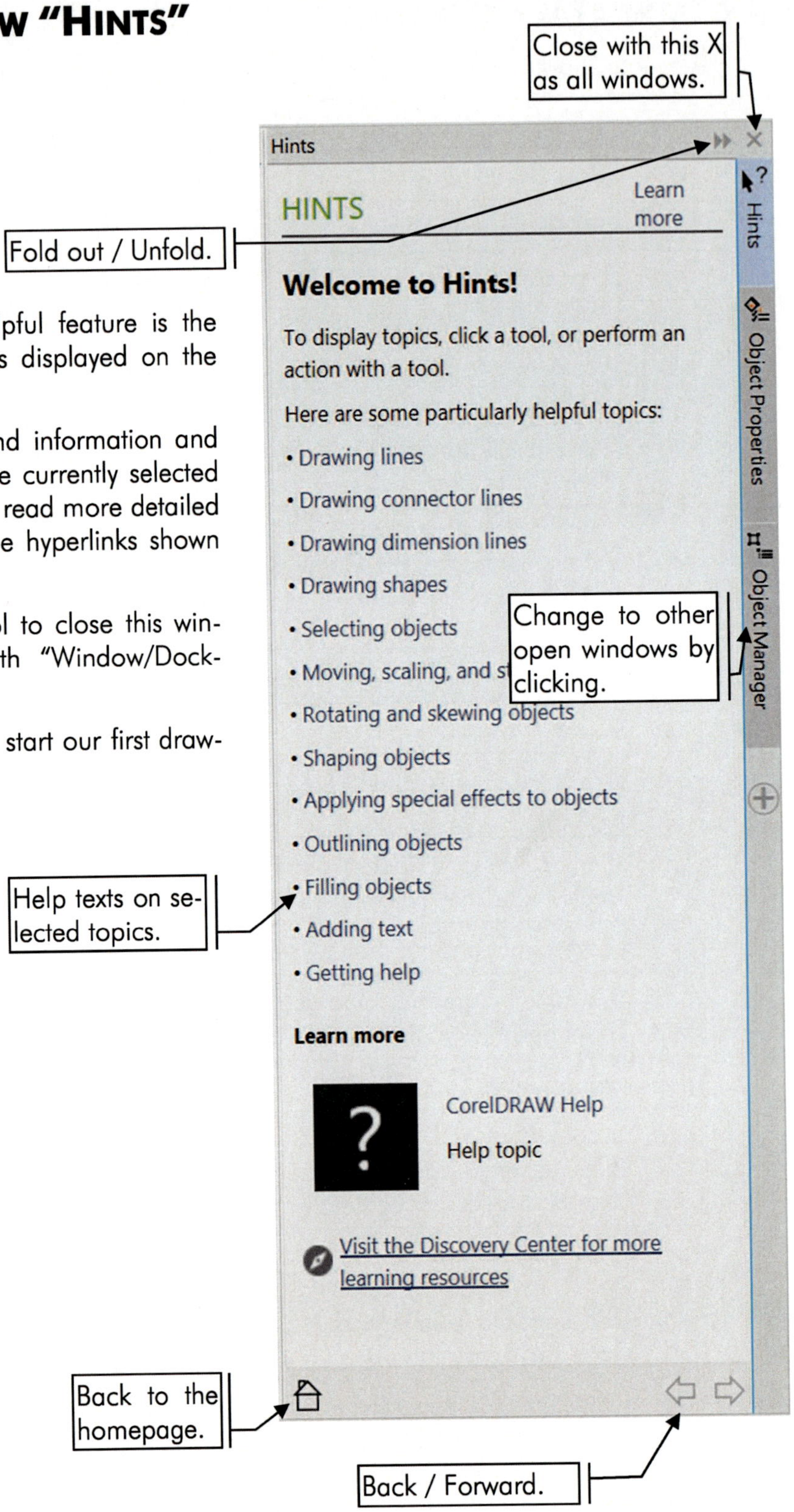

First Part

To Draw

with rectangles, ellipses, lines, colors

Looks different?
Use Window-
Workspace-Default

Chapter 3

3. First Steps

3.1 Start Corel

Start CorelDRAW from the start icon on the desktop or in the Windows start menu by "All Programs/CorelDRAW":

CorelDRAW will greet you with this welcome screen:

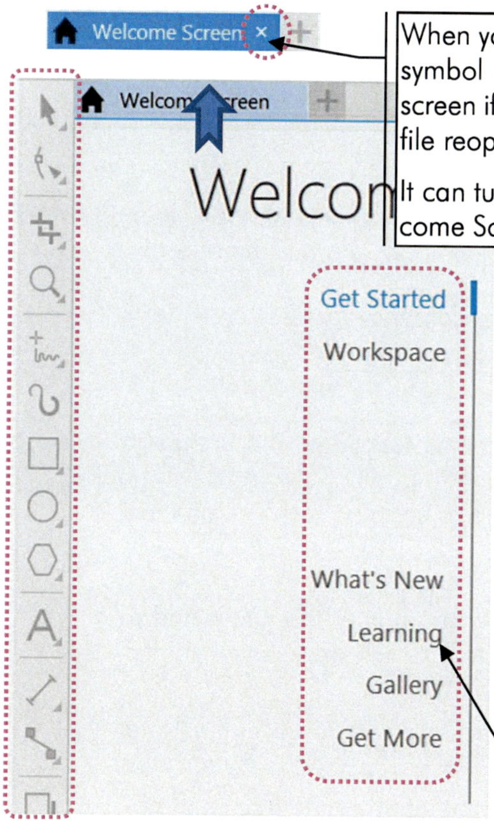

When you move the mouse over the headline, the X-symbol appears and you can close this welcome screen if you want to use the usual Windows icons for file reopening, opening or saving: 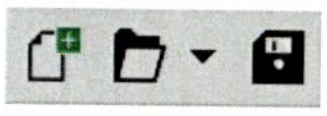

It can turned on again by the menu point Help/Welcome Screen".

- Take a look to the options What's New / Learning / Gallery / Get More.
- Start a New Document.
- Optional: New From Template or Open Document, but actually we haven't existing drawing to open so the list by Recent is empty.
  - ↳ If you have saved a drawing the last edited drawings are displayed here by Recent.

Notice the symbols. Here you find the learning tools from Corel, e.g. some training videos.

Let us begin the first drawing:

- Select a New Document in one of the ways described.
  - ↳ Without the Welcome screen above, this is the same as in any other program with the icons at the top left (new / open). 
- The appearing window for preselection, e.g. the drawing size, you can simply confirm with OK.

3.2 The Drawing Functions at a Glance

Before we start the drawing step by step, we first have a look at the drawing tools of Corel. These are located in the toolbox at the left edge:

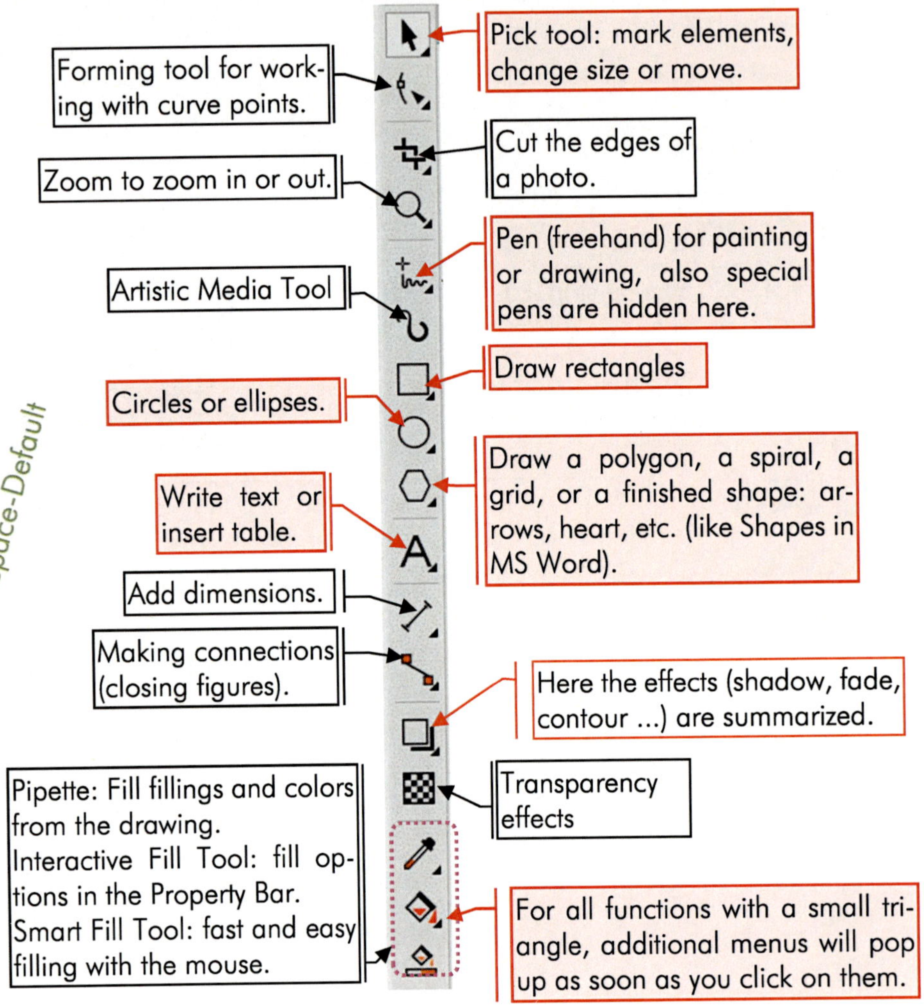

Looks different? Use Window-Workspace-Default

Note:

- If you place the mouse on a symbol for a short time, the name and a brief description of the function are reported. This is very convenient for orientation and searching for a suitable symbol.
- A description of the currently selected function is displayed in the Note window on the right side.
- If you want to draw something, first select the appropriate function (rectangle, line, etc.)!!
- If you want to change or adjust something, first select the desired object using Pick Tool.

  - ↳ Beginners often forget to switch to the pick tool and therefore draw many new mini-objects.
  - ↳ If you have drawn something inadvertently, undo it immediately, or delete it with the [Delete] key.

Accidentally drawn miniature objects complicate the selection of other objects and are often only recognizable as errors during printing!

3.3 Change, Move, Delete Rectangle

A rectangle is best suited to explaining many character functions most easily. After drawing, all elements must be pushed to the correct position and adjusted to the correct size.

Try it:

- Select Rectangle Tool, then draw a rectangle with the mouse button held.
- Immediately switch to the Pick Tool so that new rectangles are not inadvertently drawn.

The touch points appear. When the handles are visible, the rectangle is highlighted and you can position the rectangle or modify its size:

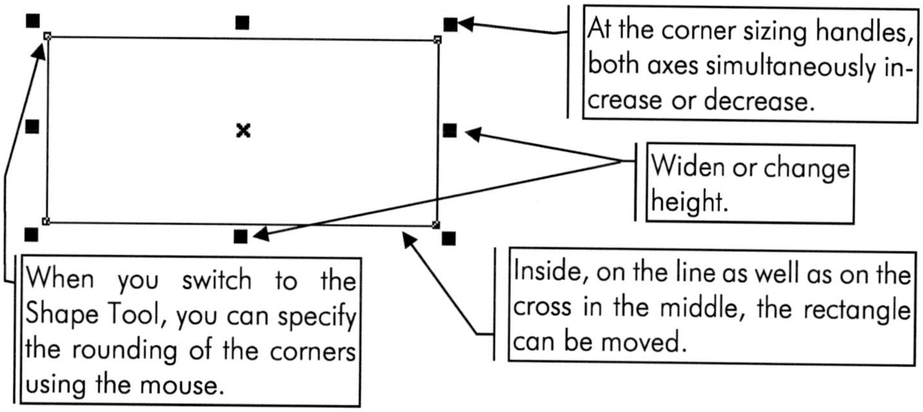

- Widen the rectangle to the right.
- Move the rectangle.
- Enlarge the rectangle on both axes at a corner sizing handle.
- Delete the rectangle: selected elements can be deleted with the [Delete] key.

To edit:

- Click the element so that the handle points appear.
  - ↳ You can change the size at the touch points, or
  - ↳ Click and hold on the item and move it, or
  - ↳ Delete the selected part with [Delete].

3.4 Rectangle Rotate or Distort

Corel provides other highly useful and very easy to use functions, e.g. to make a parallelogram from a rectangle, or to rotate it.

- Use the Pick Tool to select the object for the first time:
  - ↳ The grip points appear where the size can be changed.
- Click on the object again:
  - ↳ Arrows appear. With the arrows at the corners you can rotate, with those in the middle you can move parallel.

➢ Draw a new rectangle:

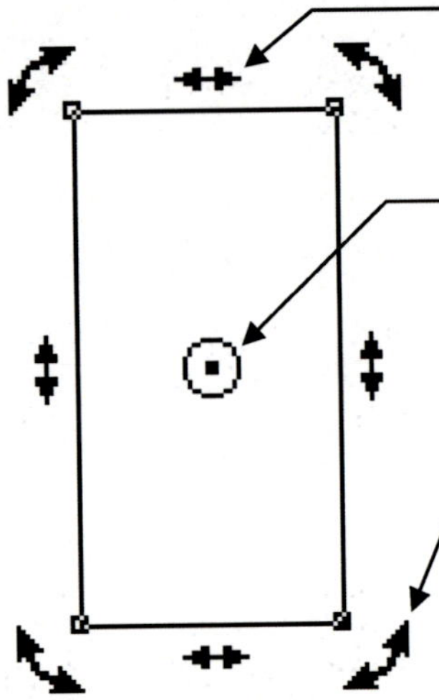

The rectangle can be moved to a parallelogram with the middle arrows. Please try!

In the middle is a small circle, which represents the pivot point. You can move this point with the mouse e.g. to a corner to make a rotation around that vertex.

The rectangle can be rotated on the corner arrows. Pressing [Ctrl] at the same time rotates in 15 ° increments (exactly 15, 30, 45, 60, 90 degrees, etc.).

➢ Try all options, draw new rectangles if necessary.

➢ Delete all rectangles.

3.4.1 SELECTION

Some symbols like the rectangle have a small triangle on the lower right. A selection menu can then be opened by holding down the left mouse button. By the rectangle, you can change options here to draw a rectangle through three points instead the usual way by holding down the left mouse button while drawing.

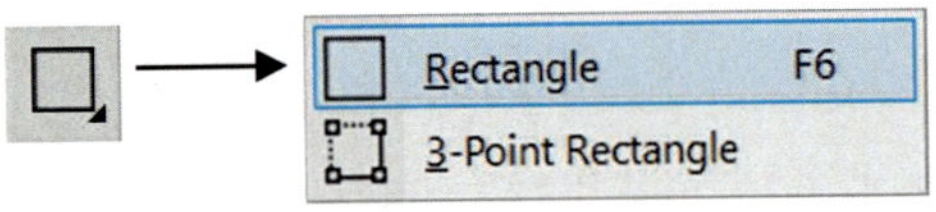

3.5 MOVE AND COPY

Drawings are labor-intensive. For example, with a wheel for a car artistically drawn, you will want to copy it and not redraw it.

Copying in Corel is very easy with a little trick:

➢ Draw a rectangle again.

Always use the Pick Tool:

- Always use the Pick Tool. Press and hold the left mouse button on the rectangle, and you can move the rectangle.
- Hold down the left mouse button, move the rectangle the same way,
  - ↳ but on the way a short click on the right mouse button and the rectangle is copied! copy
  - ↳ When you press the left mouse button, you have enough time to push the copied rectangle to the desired position.

➢ Create the following objects by copying them with the right mouse button as described above.

↳ If you hold down the [Ctrl] key, you can arrange the rectangles exactly horizontally or vertically.

Copying using the right mouse button is much easier than the normal way:

- Select Object, then Edit/Copy, the object is in memory, then Edit/Paste one or more copies or
- use the symbols:

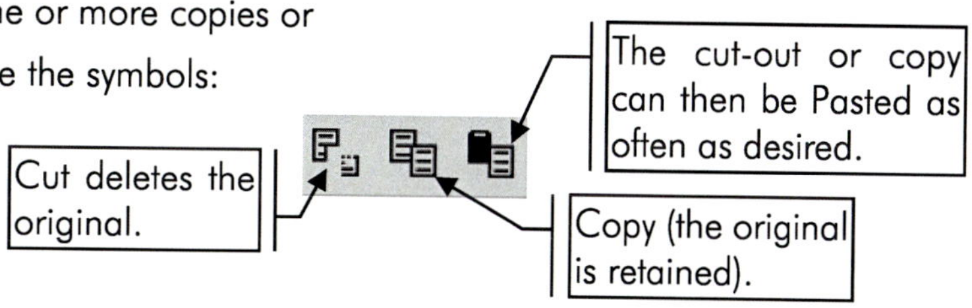

The keyboard shortcuts are another option:

[Ctrl]-X, C, V
[Ctrl]-D

- [Ctrl]-X, C, V for cut, copy or paste.

↳ C for Copy is easy to remember, the other buttons lie next to it. Otherwise, you can check the Edit Menu.

For making Duplicates you have some ways:

[Ctrl]-D

- With [Ctrl]-D or the Menu-Edit-Duplicate you get a copy.

↳ The first time you see a window where the insertion distance can be set.

↳ You can modify the duplicate distance anytime in the Property Bar if nothing is marked:

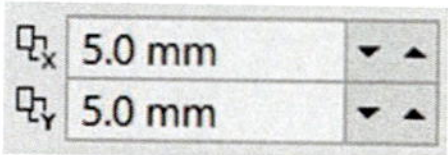

↳ But you can use Edit-Step and Repeat or Window-Dockers-Transformations-Position to make copies with specified distance.

Finishing the exercise:

➢ Finally, you can move the rectangle parallel and rotate as described above:

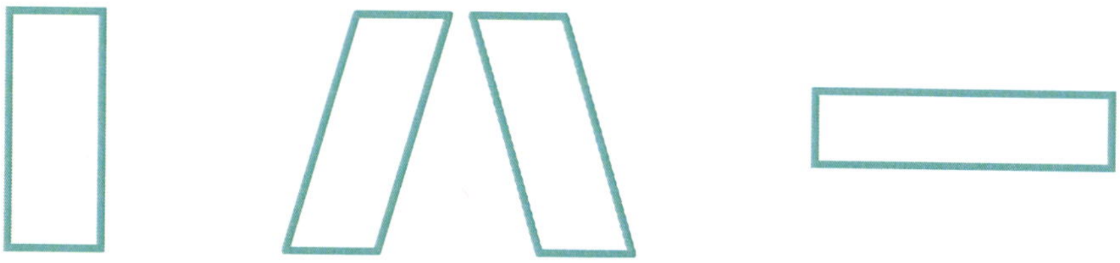

3.6 The Property Bar

Note the Property Bar, which displays the most frequently required settings, depending on the selected object, for a rectangle, e.g. the position, the size, the rounding of the corners.

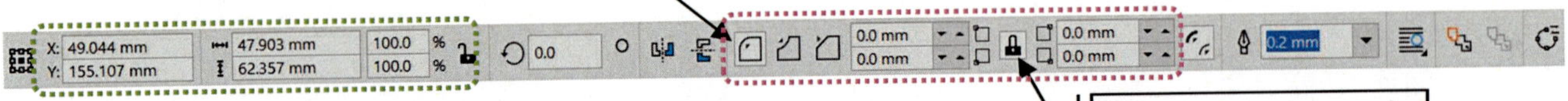

You can change all values, e.g. the width from 47.903 to 50 mm and confirm with Return or a rounding with the arrows.

When you open the lock, you can set each corner individually.

3.7 To Save

Our first exercise drawing should now be saved.

- ➢ Click on the symbol "Save".

[Ctrl]-S

We create a folder for our exercises. This goes directly in the File Save window by clicking "New Folder" (after you have chosen the left side the correct drive or folder in which you want to make a new folder, here "Documents"):

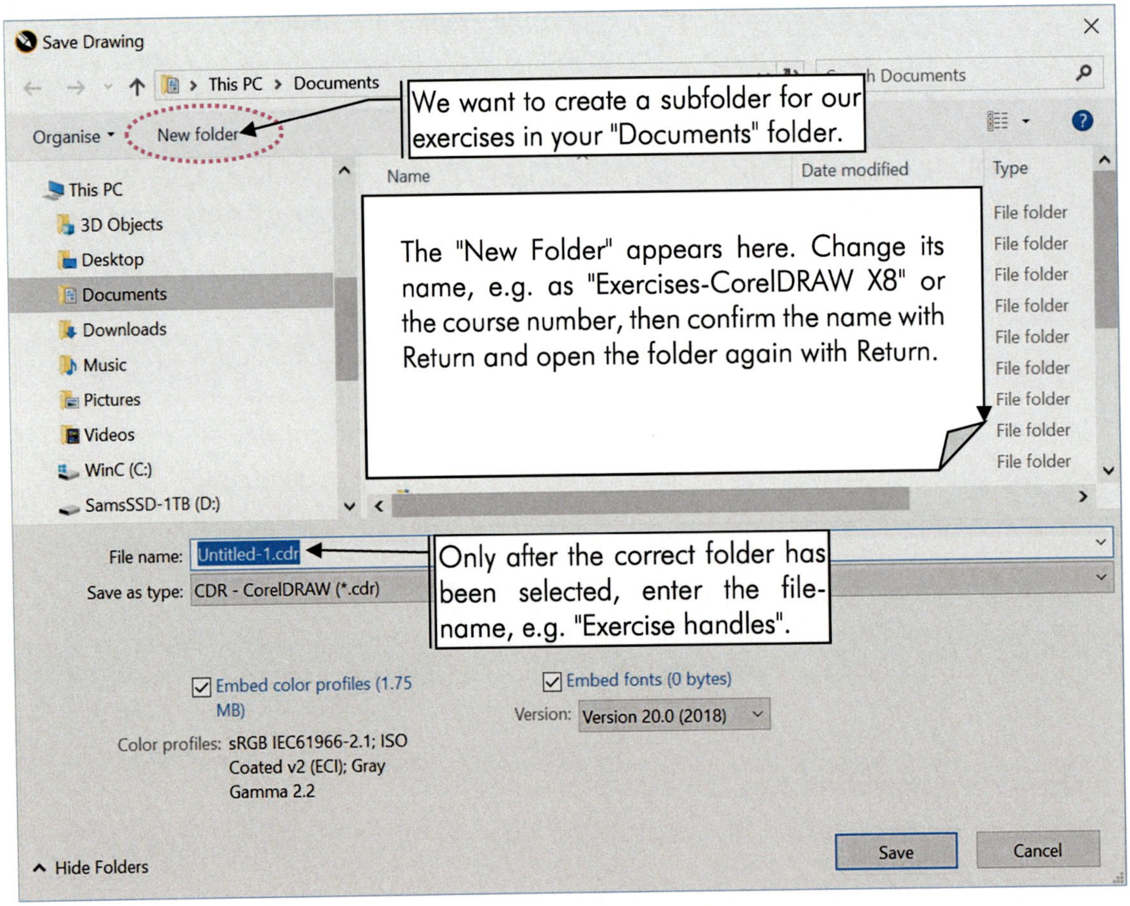

The file extension .cdr is complemented by Corel. The file transmission is not displayed by default in Windows. Graphics professionals should change this as on page 18, because with the help of the file endings, it is very easy to identify which software or photo program a file comes from.

Before each save, check these two important settings:

cdr from CorelDRAW

1. Is the correct folder selected above?
2. Does the extension fit the file name?
   - If you do not enter a file extension or a dot, Corel automatically supplements the ending cdr,
   - or leave the suffix right: filename.cdr

After saving, the new file name is displayed at the top of the CorelDRAW bar.

3.7.1 The Print

The more perfect the expression, the more minor inaccuracies occur. For the printout on a bad inkjet printer, elements can be created by eye, but for perfect printer results, it is absolutely necessary to draw perfectly from the start:

> Set the document grid and, for accurate drawing, switch on "Snap to Grid". Insert Guidelines (e.g. to mark the side edges) and activate "Snap to Guidelines".

3.7.2 The Transfer in a Print Shop

You should consider the following:

- Problems through conversion:
  - If the print shop does not have Corel, the Corel file can be converted to a different format with "File-Save as" or Export (Symbol), but conversion errors can be expected.
- File size: with photos of good quality, a project can become quite large, requiring a powerful and compatible storage medium for delivery to the print shop, if not sent by email.
  - For this purpose, USB sticks are ideal, as nowadays they have enough capacity and are more practical than burning DVDs. For larger sizes, go with USB3.0 since USB2.0 is slower.
  - Copy the used fonts and pictures as well as other used elements on these data carriers so that the printing company can postprocess the project if necessary.

Print

- Fonts: if the font should look as planned, then tell the printing company which fonts were used and also give them a copy of your fonts, too.
  - The Windows fonts are not always 100% identical on different computers, even with the same font names, depending on which source they originate from.
- If colors are to be printed exactly as planned, and are also to be reproducible every time later, use standard color palettes (e.g. Pantone) and also specify, e.g. on a separate paper the palette color numbers.

Many problems are only visible in print preparation at the print shop. It can save time when the printer has all the elements used. In any case, you should talk to the printing company about your plans at an early stage, if possible with printouts, and also how the data should be delivered to the printing company.

You can only create professional printouts in a print shop.

Chapter 4

4. Ellipses, Select, Colors

4.1 The CorelDraw Construction

At the top is the command menu File ..., selected commands as icons in the toolbar, and the Properties bar. Notice: this is with workspace default.

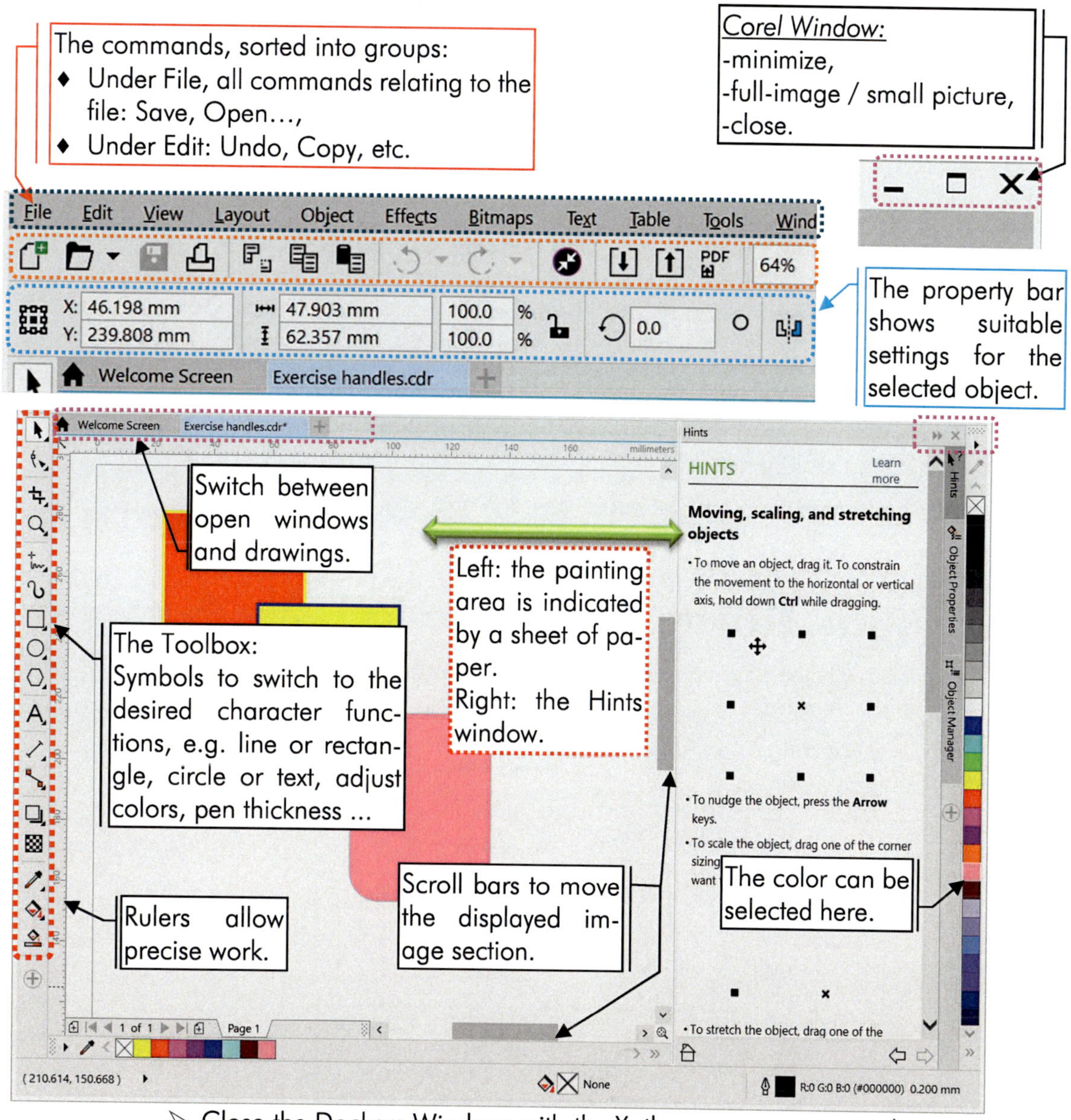

➢ Close the Dockers Windows with the X, they consume too much space. You can turn them on again with Window/Dockers….

4.2 Set up the Page

For this new drawing, DIN A4 portrait format is not suitable. We therefore want to set the paper format to DIN A5 transversely. This will be in the dialog box, which appears after "new file" as well as at any time in the Property Bar (if nothing is marked). We recommend not using the dialog box to change the page format later in the drawing.

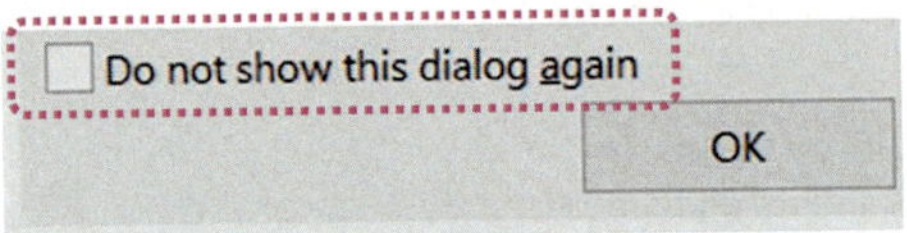

- ➢ Start a new document.
- ➢ Turn off the New Document Window permanently.
  - ➭ You can reactivate every time as follows: Tools/Options/General: "Show New Document dialog box".
- ➢ If nothing is selected, the page settings (paper size, etc.) are displayed in the property bar.
  - ➭ Click with the pick tool in the empty area, so that nothing is marked.

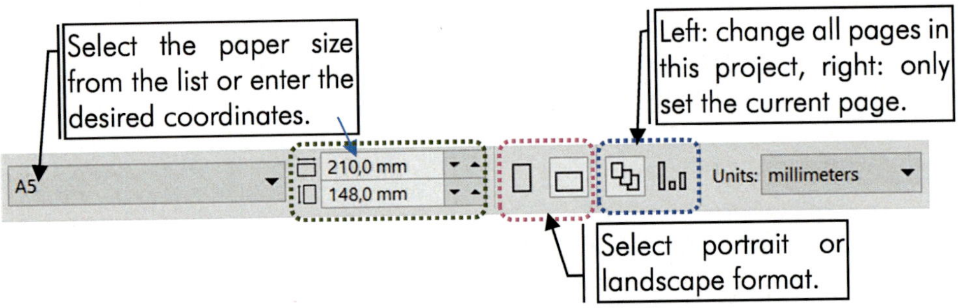

- ➢ You can also set the page size in the Layout-Page Setup menu. You should have a look at this menu.
- ♦ For layout, you will also find the Page Background command.
  - ➭ In this menu, you can easily select a color or an image as the background of the page.
  - ➭ The bitmap size must be same as page size; if it's smaller, you get tiles.

4.3 Rectangles, Ellipses, Variety

- ➢ Now draw some rectangles and ellipses. The lowest symbol can be used to select the shapes.
- ➢ Save as "Rectangles and Ellipses".

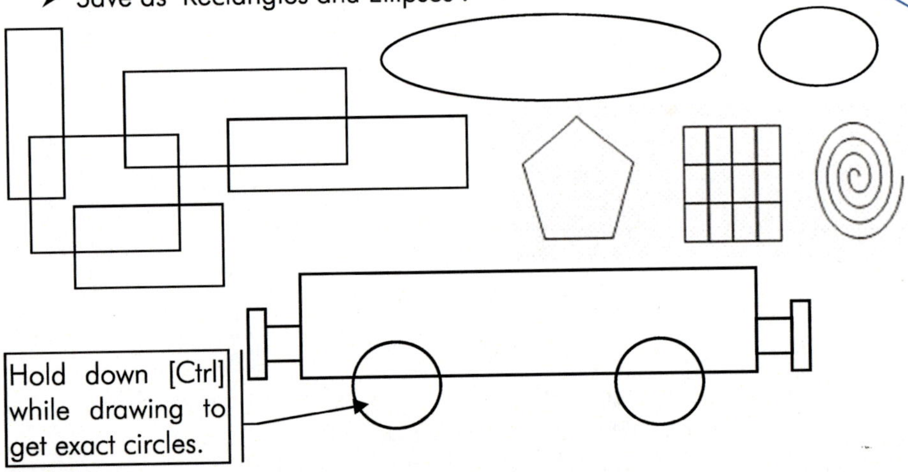

4.4 MARKING AND MOVING

The drawn objects may not fit optimally to the new paper size. No problem:

One object:

- Click on the selection arrow to select it.
  - ↳ The touch points appear so that the size can be changed, etc.

Several objects:

- Can be clicked and selected by holding down the [Shift] key.
  - ↳ Note the message at the bottom of the status line: "X Objects selected...", otherwise it did not work.
- With the selection tool you can drag a large frame, just like a rectangle, except that the selection arrow is a marking frame.

  Marking frame

  - ↳ All objects within this frame are highlighted and can now be moved, copied, deleted, and so on.
- You can also select Edit/Select All/Objects (text, guidelines or nodes).

Exercise: Moving and Resize

- ➢ Select all drawn objects with a marking frame,
- ➢ then move all at once, either
  - ↳ use the mouse to touch a line or
  - ↳ with the directional buttons, very precisely, or
  - ↳ specify the new coordinates in the property bar.

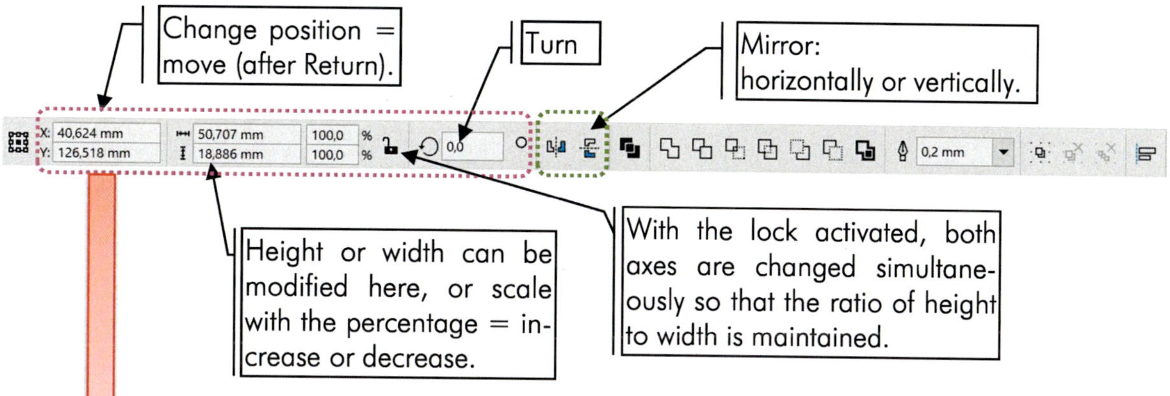

Note:

- The upper row changes the X-axis, or the width.
- The lower row changes the Y-axis or the height.

Notes: ....

....

....

....

4.5 Select Colors

The rectangles are in simple black but somewhat bland. Let us make it colorful. Colors can be selected via the color palette at the right edge of the screen.

- First, mark an object, e.g. a rectangle.
- Then, the color for the selected object can be changed. Just click on a color of the color palette on the right margin.

4.6 The Color Palette

Only a few colors are displayed in the visible area of the color palette. The other colors are as follows:

Change to other pallets and various commands.

The X for turned off, means without filling or an invisible frame line.

Turn On color palette

From Black to Grey to White, then follows the other colors.

- If the color palette is turned off:
  - You can activate it again by Window/Color Palettes.
  - The default is the "default palette", we'll look at the other palettes below.

With the left mouse button as fill color, Right-click the line color.

Attention! If nothing is selected, you will change the defaults. Cancel if warning window appears!

The color palette contains even more colors. Use these arrows to move the visible range or

Herewith display the complete color palette.

➢ Assign a line and fill color to all drawn elements.
  - In this case, too, you can select several elements with the [Shift] key or with a marking frame and assign a color to it at once.

The fill and line color of the active object is displayed at the bottom right:

The lines are still very thin. This can also be changed.

4.7 Changing Line Thickness

In order for the outlines to become more visible, we can increase the line thickness with the line icon in the Property Palette:

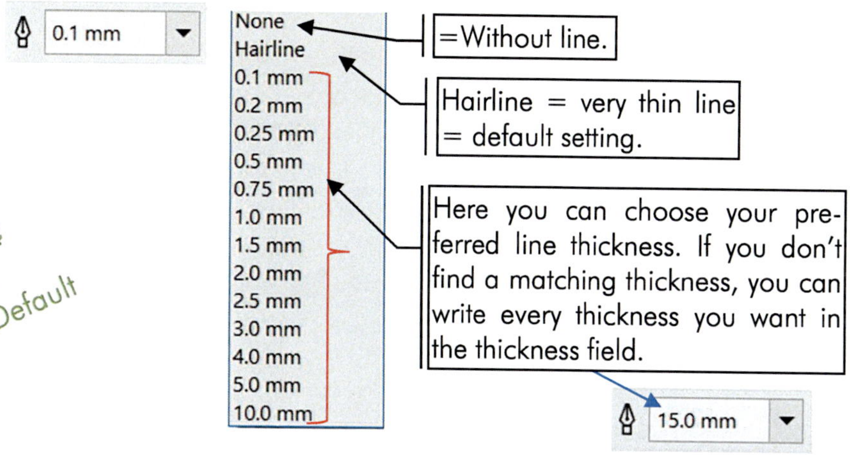

Looks different? Use Window-Workspace-Default

- Window/Dockers/Object Properties or right mouse button on the object and Object Properties opens all settings.
  - ✎ Expand the menu with the small arrow if necessary:

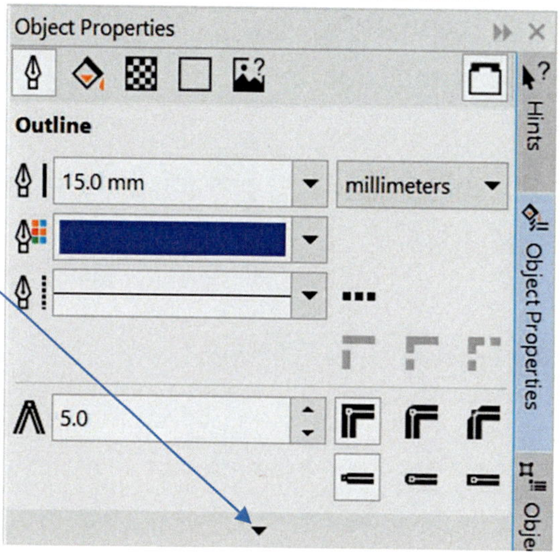

- ➢ Use a large marking frame to select several objects and change the line thickness.
- ➢ Then, change the line and fill colors again.

It could be so colorful:

Do the wheels disappear behind the box? If not, the remedy follows on the next page.

4.8 The Property Bar – Position

- In Corel, what was drawn last is front. If this is filled, everything underneath is hidden. If you have drawn the wheels last, they should be placed behind the car.
  - ↳ Instead of marking two wheels, it is easier to mark the car and move it forward.
- ➢ Right mouse button on the object, then Order:

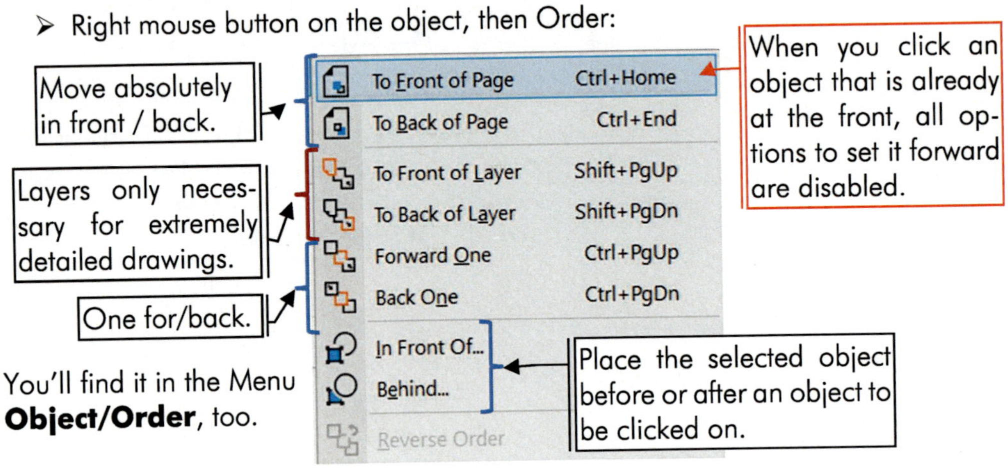

You'll find it in the Menu **Object/Order**, too.

- ➢ Now select the polygon, set it to the front and set a different number of corners.

4.9 Undo

- With the following advice, nothing bad can happen to your project:
  - ↳ Observe the result on the screen for each action.
  - ↳ If the expected has not been entered, select Undo immediately.
  - ↳ Find the cause (wrong command, not marked, etc.) and find the correct command.

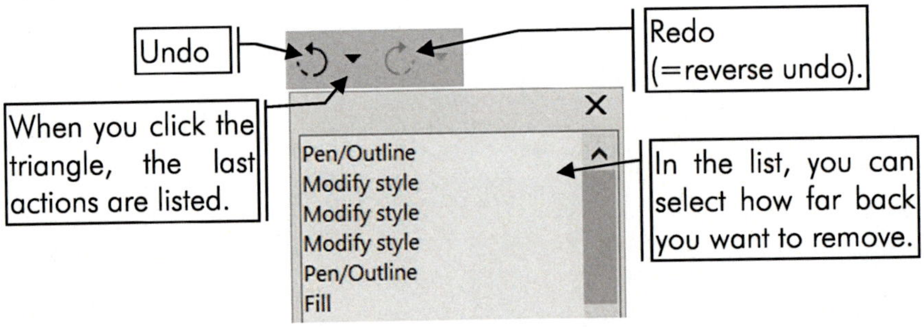

4.9.1 Delete

Of course, you can also simply delete objects that are not fitting:

- ➢ Click with the Pick Tool on the object to be deleted.
  - ↳ Here, too, it is often convenient to select several elements with a selection frame or with the [Shift] key pressed.
- ➢ When the object is highlighted, which is recognizable by the appearing touch points, press the [Delete] key.

Chapter 5

5. Zoom and View

If you expand your frame so that you can see the entire current drawing area well, many mistakes can be avoided from the outset, e.g. non-matching lines.

5.1 Zoom with the Zoom Tool

There are several ways to zoom. The simplest way is as follows:

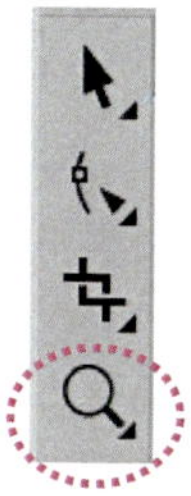

- Choose the Zoom Tool on the left side.
  - ↳ You can now use the mouse to zoom:
    left mouse button = zoom in
    right mouse button = zoom out
    or draw a marking rectangle by holding down the mouse button.
  - ↳ Or use the icons in the property bar to zoom in or out (appears when the Zoom Tool is selected):

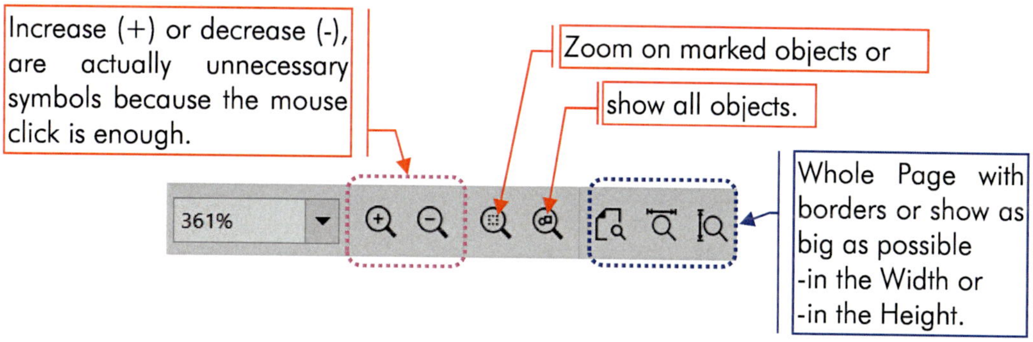

- With a Wheel Mouse you can scroll in/out with the mouse wheel also if the Zoom Tool is not selected and
  - ↳ The panning modus can start by clicking the wheel.

The Panning modus:

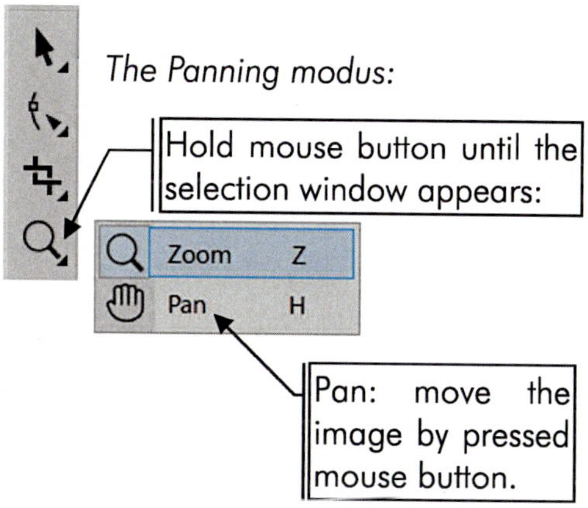

Note the following Shortcuts:

- [F3] = zoom out
- [F4] = zoom all objects
- [F9] preview on whole screen, back with [Esc] or mouse click.

5.2 THE ZOOM BUTTON

The Zoom button is located not only in the Property Bar when the Zoom tool is selected, it is also always in the Standard Bar:

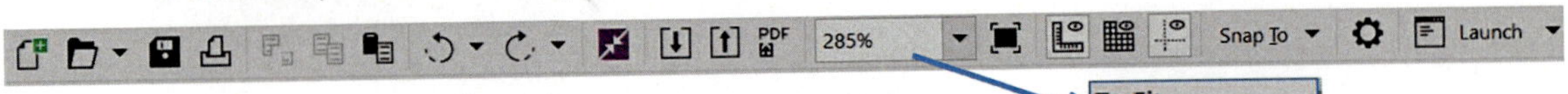

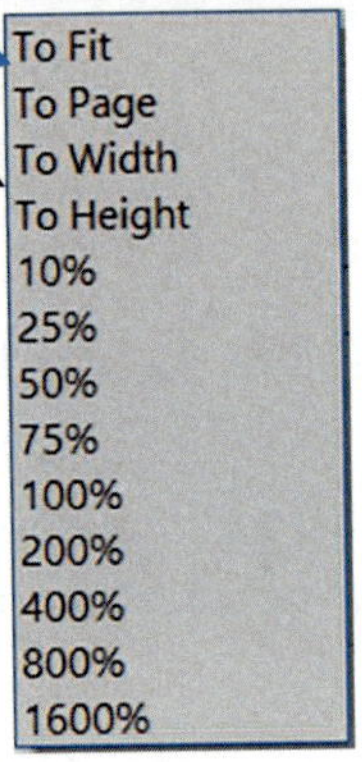

For example, with "To Width", the drawing is displayed as wide as possible.

Various zoom levels are available again.

F4

To Fit: As with [F4], all drawn elements are displayed as large as possible.

5.3 SETTING THE DISPLAY

This information is presented here only because it can cause major problems, e.g. no fillings are displayed. In View, you can choose:

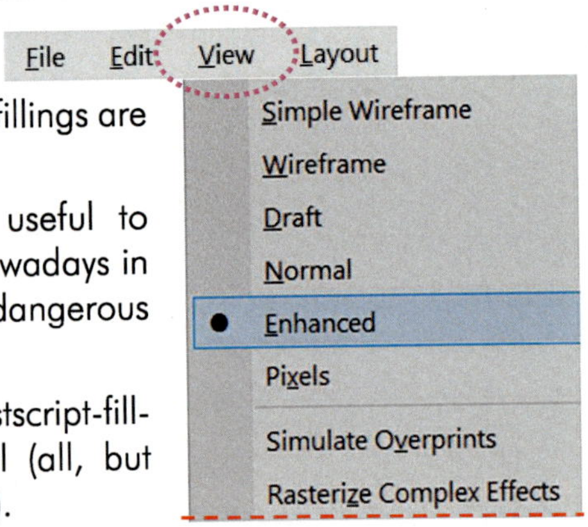

- For Wireframe, only outlines, but no fillings are displayed.
  - ✎ Previously this was sometimes useful to speed up the image build-up, nowadays in case of accidental switching, a dangerous option!
- Usually the display is Enhanced (postscript-fillings displayed detailed) or Normal (all, but postscript-fillings displayed shadowy).
- Pixels: with a higher zoom you see the pixels. But it is not as really printed. So, it uses only as much as the capacity of your computer and graphics card.
- Simulate Overprints – with Offset printing it is unfavourable if a bright object is printed over a dark one – this case can be displayed here.
- Rasterize Complex Effects: it can help by printing problems if complex effects are output like photos as pixel patterns.

In the View Menu, you will find these interesting functions:

- Page Sorter View: Before printing once again, see all pages. To turn it off, select it again or press [Esc].
- Grid, Rulers, Guidelines: you can switch it on or off. Just try the grid for now, an explanation follows in the next chapter.
- Page: here you can e.g. make the "Printable Area" visible. This means the area where your printer can print is, most of the time, a little smaller than the page.
  - ✎ Page Border displays the set paper size so you can arrange the drawing elements appropriately (default is on).

5.4 Settings of CorelDraw

- By Tools/Options you can change the presets of the Corel program.
  - ✎ By Tools/Customization you come to the same menu only with the difference that the point Customization is selected.
- With Tools/Save Settings as Default you can save the current drawing settings as a general preset.

This method also allows you to save the most commonly used paper size, as well as the grid and guideline settings, as the default for all new drawings.

5.5 Switch the Command Bars on or off

Looks different? Use Window-Workspace-Default

You can also turn on additional toolbars, for example, the Text Toolbar for font settings, or accidentally deactivated toolbars by Tools/Customization/Command Bars.

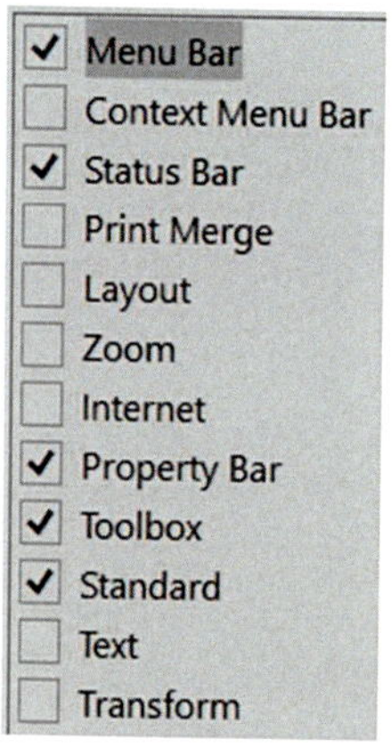

Overview Command Bars:

- The Menu Bar contains File, Edit, View ...

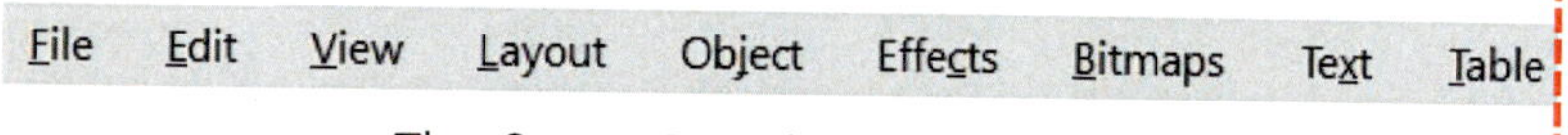

- The Status Bar shows additional information at the bottom of the Corel window.

- The Standard Bar is the most used bar at the top with New File, Open, Save, Print

- Below is the Property Bar (symbols change, depending on what is selected):

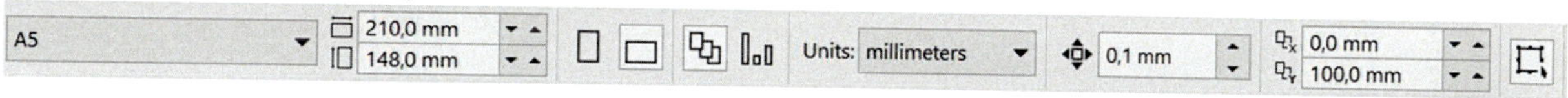

- Toolbox: the command symbols on the left side with the drawing tools:

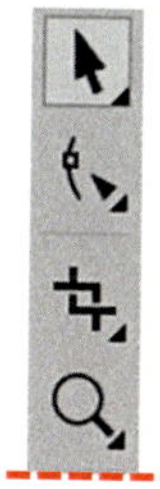

Exercise: Command Bars:

➢ Turn on deactivated command bars, view them and turn them off again.
  - ✎ You can see the effect directly on the screen without having to leave the menu.

The toolbars are initially fixed and cannot be moved. In the Tools/Customization Menu or on a bar, press the right mouse button (at the edge, not on a symbol), then deactivate "Lock toolbars".

➢ Drag the Toolbox into the drawing and reshape the tool palette at the edges, as soon as the mouse changes to a double arrow.

➢ Close the Toolbox. Now turn on the Toolbox and push it to the old position (do not release the mouse too early).
  - ✎ Finally, click the right mouse button and choose Look Toolbars again.

Chapter 6

6. Lines

6.1 Freehand Tool

Lines are drawn with the Freehand Tool. There are several possibilities. We start with the freehand line.

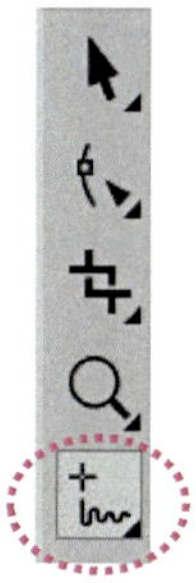

- ➢ Freehand Tool: New drawing on DIN A4 transversely, then select the Freehand Tool and press the mouse button to draw:
- ➢ The lines are rounded automatically, fewer turning points facilitate subsequent shaping. More about curve processing on page 99.

> If you want to draw a lot of freehand, you should consider the purchase of a drawing tablet with a pressure-sensitive pencil, because the mouse is not suitable for freehand drawing. With such a pen the line becomes thicker when you press harder.

- ➢ Complete the drawing by switching to the Pick Tool and setting a different color as well as a thicker line.

Not only freehand lines, even straight lines and polygons are possible.

6.1.1 Straight Lines

- ➢ For a straight line with the line tool:
  - ➷ First mouse click = starting point,
  - ➷ Click elsewhere = end point.

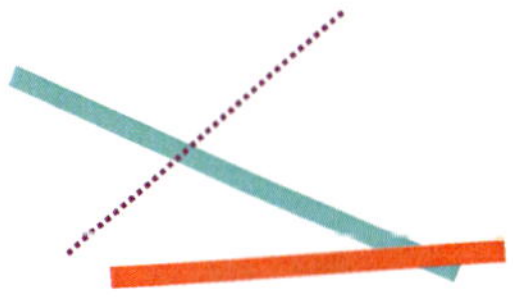

6.1.2 Polygon

- ♦ The line tool can be used to continue a straight line:
  - ➷ First mouse click = starting point, then move the mouse away.
  - ➷ Double-click will set a point, but the line continues, so you can add with double-click as many lines as you want.
  - ➷ Until you set the end point with one click.
- ➢ Draw a triangle or a carnival cap!

6.2 Lines in an Angle

Horizontal or vertical lines or lines at the following angles: 15°, 30°, 45°, 60°, 90° etc. can be drawn in this easy way:

➢ Set the start point as usual, move the mouse away, and hold down the [Ctrl] key.

↳ If you rotate the mouse pointer around the starting point, you can see that the line is drawn only at these angles.

➢ Drag a horizontal line across the entire page:

6.3 Exercise Lines

➢ Draw the following in your drawing, then save as "lines and shapes":

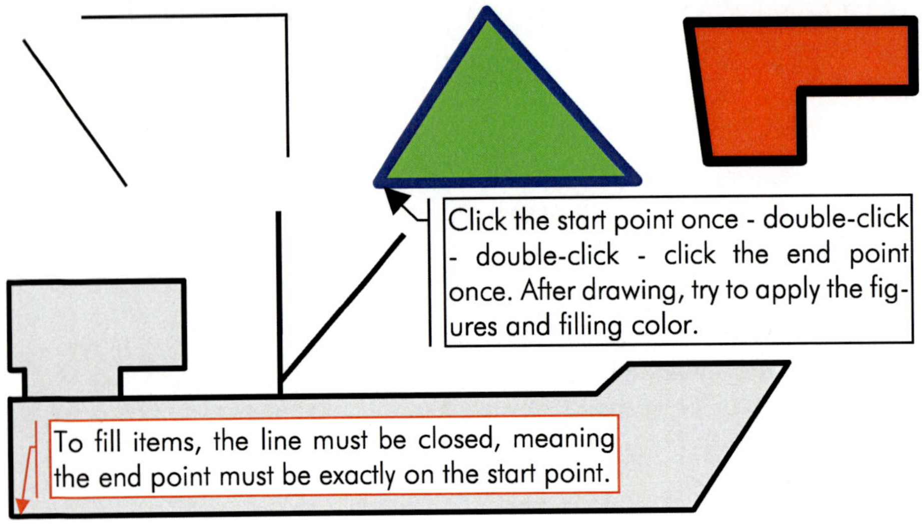

6.4 Exercise Convertible

➢ New drawing on DIN A5 transversally and save as convertible.

➢ Draw a horizontal line as a road, draw a wheel as a circle (hold down the [Ctrl] key), set a thick line for the tire, and a matching fill color.

➢ Copy this circle when finished, for the second wheel, and also arrange it above the road line.

➢ Draw the chassis out of closed lines (double-click), then select a Fill Color and move backwards (right mouse button – order, or [Ctrl]-Page down) so that the wheels are in front. The symbols disappear if more than one object is selected.

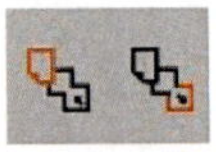

[Ctrl]-Page up/down

➢ Finally, draw the front disc as a triangle of lines, fill and set to the body of the car.

6.5 Pencil Types

If you hold the mouse on the freehand pin tool, you can switch to additional line types in the menu that appears:

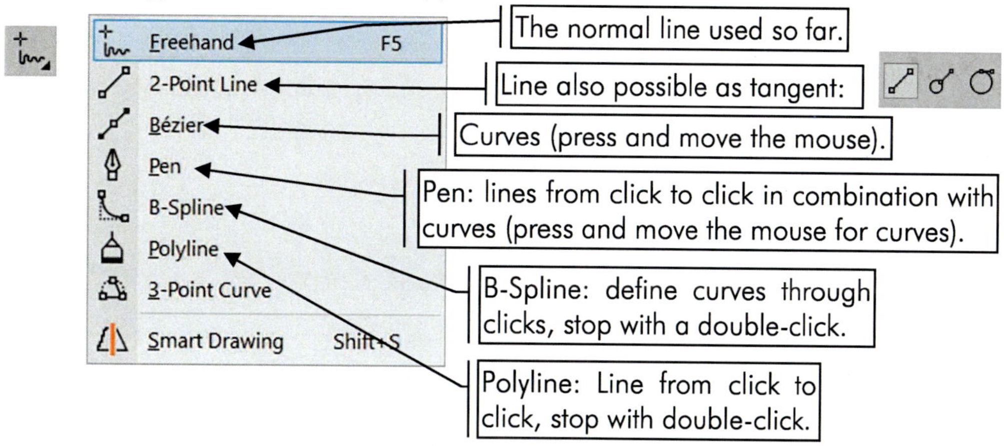

Instead the "Bezier, B-Spline, 3-Point-Curve" curves are easier to create and adjust with curve processing. See details on page 99. So, in this menu only the Freehand line and the Polyline are recommended.

6.6 Artistic Media Tools

Among the pen types is the Artistic Media Tool with a variety of fascinating and interesting drawing features.

➢ Start a new drawing and choose the Artistic Media Tool. In the Property Bar you will now find the following setting options:

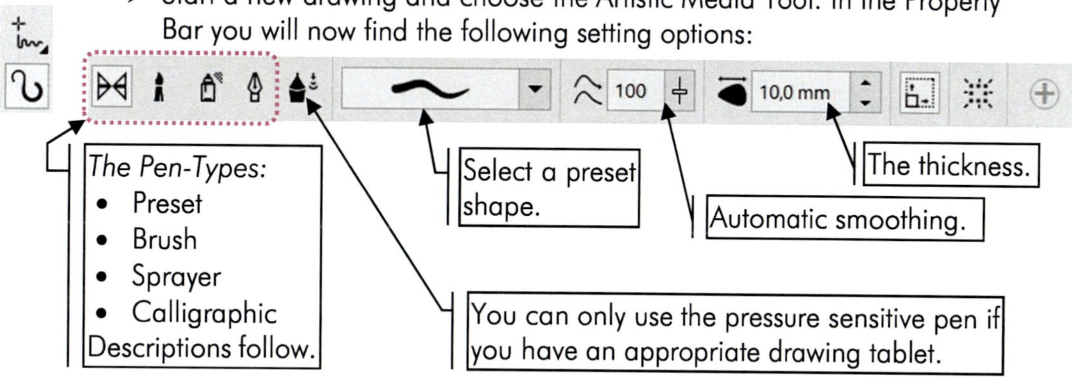

With Effects/Artistic Media, you will find these pen types again as docking windows. Select pencil type and shape, then paint. However, you can also change the shape after the object is selected or even assign the shapes to other drawn elements. For example, mark a rectangle, then select a preset line shape or an image spray can.

6.6.1 Artistic Media Tools - Preset

Instead of a line of uniform width, you can select specific line shapes, e.g. a wedge-shaped line or a water droplet.

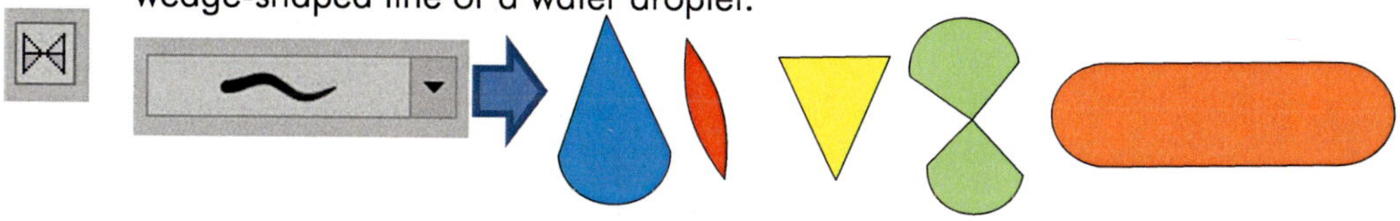

6.6.2 Artistic Media Tools - Brush

These brushes paint beautiful wallpaper patterns on the page.

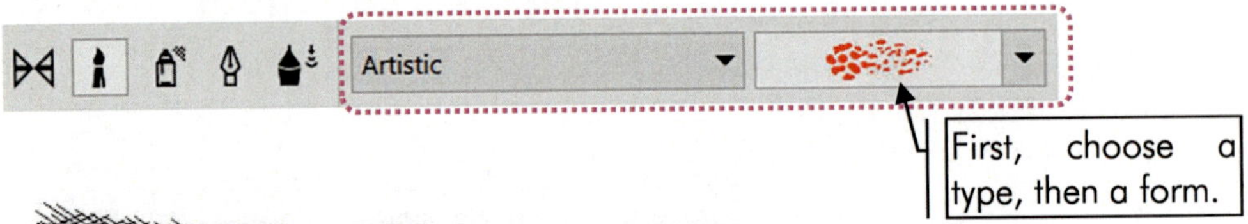

6.6.3 Artistic Media Tools - Sprayer

With the Sprayer you can spray a series of images with the mouse button pressed down. Try some types using the two selection buttons:

6.6.4 Artistic Media Tools - Calligraphic

If you paint sideways with a wide brush, the line is quite thin, but crosswise wide. This gives the calligraphic effects (e.g. when painting Chinese or Japanese characters). You can simulate such brush strokes with this function, whereby the width of the brush and the rotation can be specified.

- Draw a Japanese letter, first increase the angle for a flat brush to 60 °.

6.7 Exercise Pen

- Paint with the Pen Tool the boat (straight lines), two rectangles for the blue sky and the darker water (fill blue), head and body as ellipses, and hair with the pen.
- The rest (clouds, balloons, waves ...) are brush or sprayer effects.

6.8 Smart Fill Tool

The Smart Fill Tool allows you to fill in intersections:

- Draw a rectangle and circle and try it out.

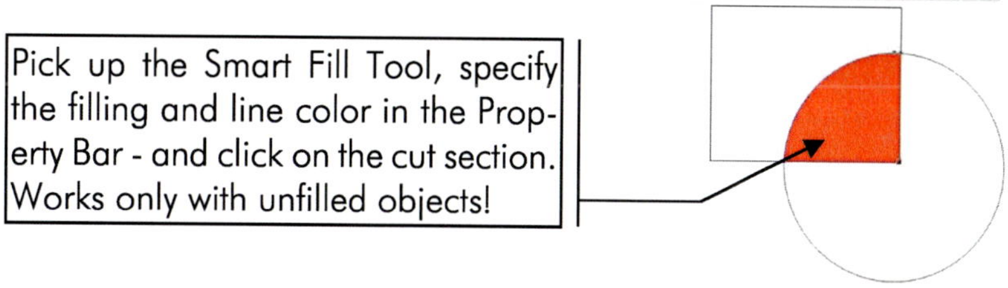

6.9 Smart Drawing

In the Pen Menu, you can select the Smart Drawing Tool:

[Shift]-S

If the Smart Drawing Tool is activated, you can draw with a pressed left mouse button and Corel will try to complete and close a form (rectangle, circle, polygon...). Try it:

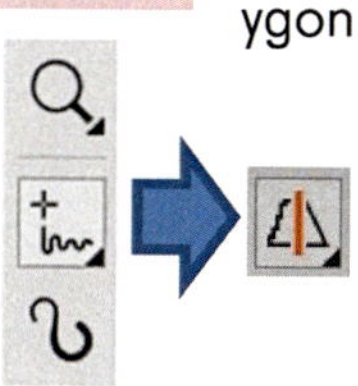

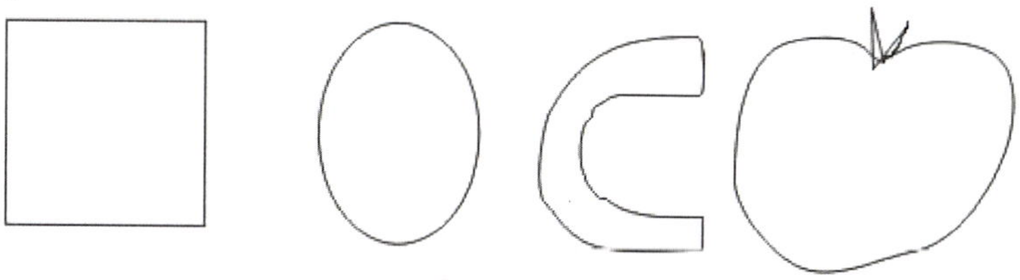

Second Part

Precise Drawing

Square, Circle, Grid, Guidelines, Text, Group

Chapter 7

7. PRECISE DRAWING

7.1 THE GRID

The Grid is a useful aid in precise drawing.

- For example, if the Grid is activated, aligned, and set to a distance of 5 mm, all newly drawn parts are arranged on this 5 mm grid.
  - ➯ Crawling measures, such as the line 45,05756 / 33,45666, are thus avoided from the outset and can be accurately drawn without any effort.

The grid can be set up in several ways. The best method is with the right mouse button on the ruler, then "Grid Setup...".

It is always the same menu for the settings, which can be opened via the Tools/Options/Grids or by the right mouse-button on the ruler:

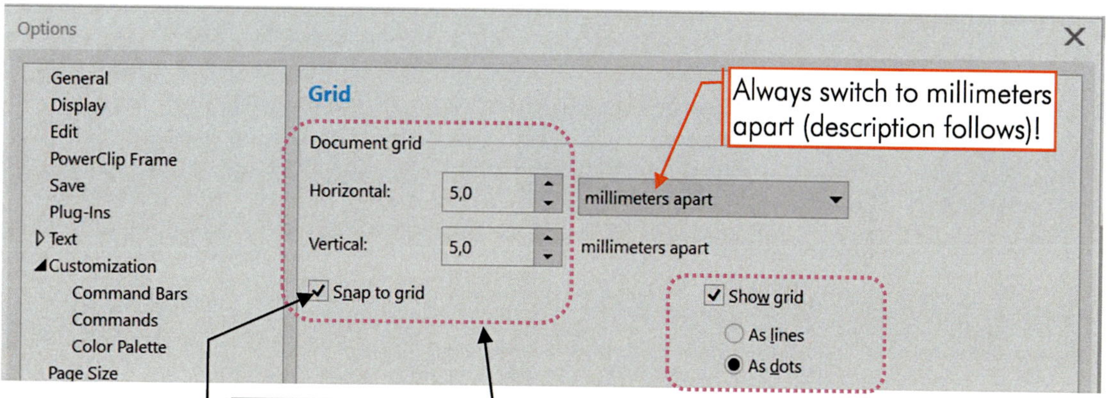

In addition, you should also have them aligned with the help lines.

Whether you want to see the grid is a matter of taste, but aligning with the grid should be activated in any case, except when drawing freehand.

More with the grid:

- With View/Grid you can show or hide the grid points,
- With View/Snap to you can activate or deactivate the alignment of the various grids or guidelines.

[Ctrl]-Y

  - ➯ Baseline Grid: Horizontal help lines similar to lined paper are displayed in the set point distance.
  - ➯ Guidelines: Sometimes, it is not enough to draw help lines into the drawing. Only when this is activated is the entire image also aligned with help lines.

Notes on the grid:

- 0.2 grid lines per millimeter = grid points every 5 millimeters.
- The grid points are automatically displayed with some space between.
  - ↳ If the view is very reduced, Corel removes the grid points so that a black drawing full of grid points is not displayed.

7.1.1 EXERCISE: PYRAMIDS FROM SQUARES

Draw the following pyramid from squares.

[Ctrl]

- ➢ New drawing, DIN A5 crosswise, adjust the grid to a distance of 10 mm.
- ➢ Then draw a square (hold down [Ctrl] key or use the grid) and copy multiple times using the mouse:
  - ↳ Move and click the right mouse button on the way, and release the left button at the destination.
- When drawing, moving, and reshaping, note whether the cursor jumps to the grid points (if necessary, touch the corner).
  - ↳ If not, check to see if the grid is activated, the distance is correct, and the Alignment is set to On.

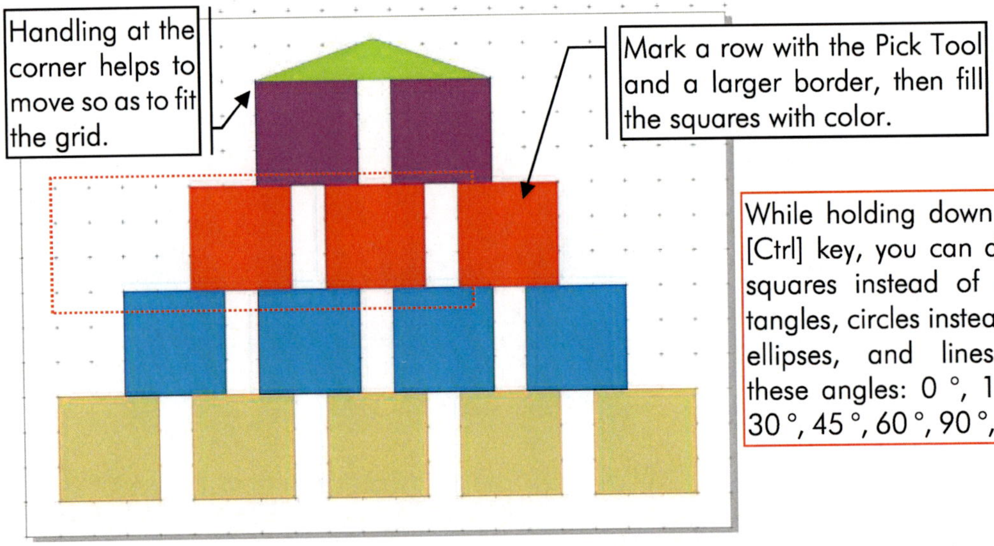

While holding down the [Ctrl] key, you can draw squares instead of rectangles, circles instead of ellipses, and lines at these angles: 0 °, 15 °, 30 °, 45 °, 60 °, 90 °, etc.

- ➢ Save this exercise as "pyramid squares", as this is reused later.

7.1.2 FURTHER ON THE GRID

Now we've set up the grid and can draw with it exactly. At least the good expression makes the change hardly noticeable.

- If you draw a detail greatly enlarged, you can fine-tune the grid, by every millimeter or even every 0.1 mm.
- The grid is optimal and should always be used, so that everything fits effortlessly. The only exceptions are genuine freehand drawings.

> For freehand elements (curves, stars, figures, etc.) the grid would only interfere: with [Ctrl]-Y, temporarily switch off the grid feature.

7.2 Copy and Move

[Ctrl]-D

- You can also create a copy using the Edit/Duplicate command (make sure you specify the insertion distance for the first time).
- If the Pick Tool is active a selected Element can be moved precisely with the directional buttons in the property bar.

  ⇘ But if no object is selected (if necessary, click with the Pick Tool in an empty area), the step size can be set there:

The step width when moving with the directional buttons can be adjusted at any time - Practical for precise and easy moving.

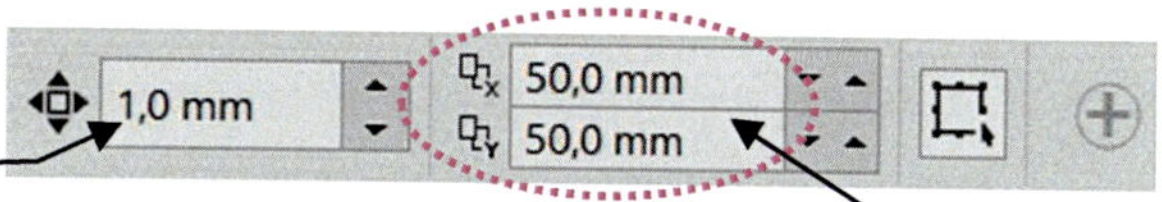

Space between duplicates.

The default setting:

➢ You can specify the step size in the property bar, or by Tools/Options/Rulers.

⇘ For example, at 1 mm, you can move the elements marked with the direction buttons by 1 mm each. The larger step size applies when the [Shift] key is pressed, e.g. you could specify 10 for 10x1mm here.

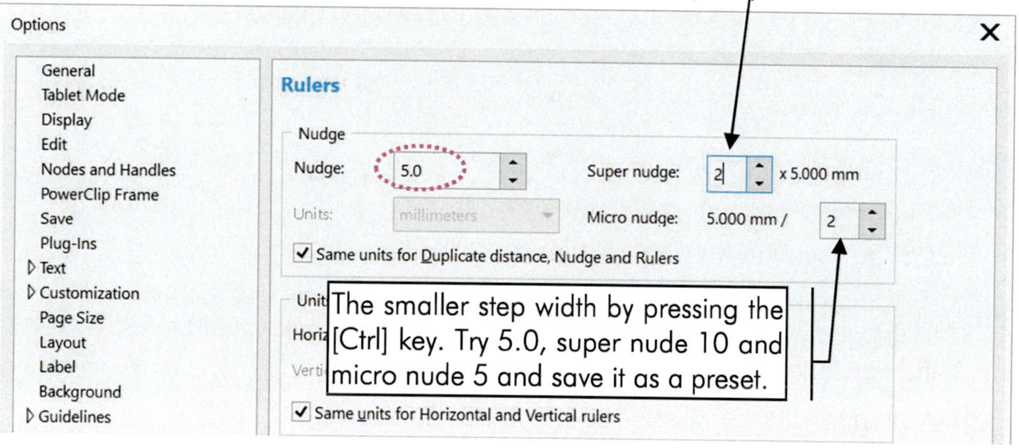

7.3 Exercise

➢ Create rectangles and lines using copy, then rotate and move them to make the following farm. Make the work easier by increasing as much as you draw.

Draw once, copy often.

7.4 Guidelines Setup

The question remains: how are objects are easier to arrange at the same height? With the guidelines.

Important notes about the guidelines:

- Guidelines are not printed, but the objects can be aligned exactly on these lines. Guidelines are therefore optimal to specify page margins or to arrange elements flush.
- Rulers/Grid/Guidelines visible/invisible: 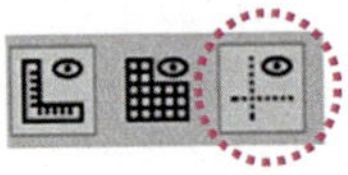

7.4.1 Set Guidelines and Move

The rulers are located at the top and left.

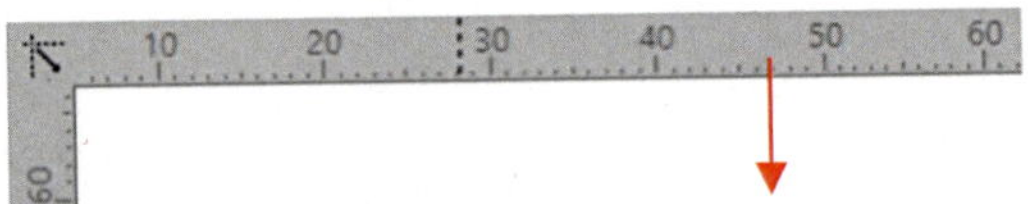

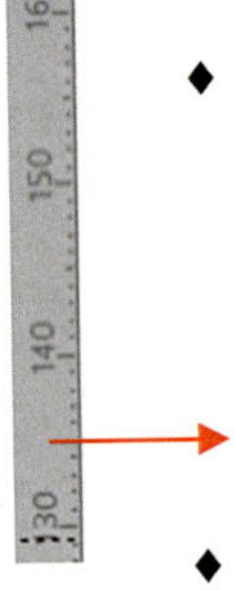

- Pull with the left mouse button from the ruler into the drawing - a guideline is there.
  - ↳ Pulling from the horizontal Ruler you can pull horizontal guidelines into the drawing.
  - ↳ Pulling from the vertical Ruler you can pull vertical guidelines into the drawing.
- Delete Guidelines: click on the guideline and press [Del].

Exercise:

- ➢ Start a new drawing, again DIN A5-cross.
- ➢ First, align your grid with lines every 5mm.
  - ↳ If you now draw guidelines into the drawing, they will also be aligned to the grid as long as you release the mouse near a grid point (note the appearing marks).
- ➢ Then drag two horizontal and two vertical guides as a side-edge marker into the drawing.

Move Guidelines:

- ➢ Try to move a vertical and a horizontal help line: click and drag them to another location.

Now we turn a Guideline:

- ➢ Pull another guideline in the middle of it. When clicking on it, the arrows on which the guideline can be rotated appear outside.
  - ↳ You can also specify the angle of rotation in the property bar (confirm with Return). Right of the angle you can set the center of rotation.

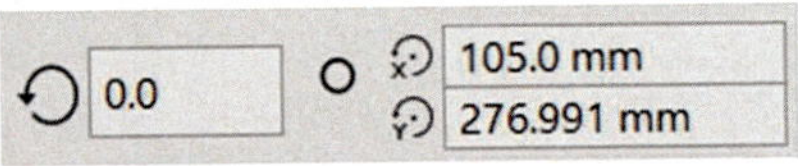

- The guideline menu is useful when many help lines are set:
  - ↳ To open the menu, double click on a guideline or
  - ↳ Right mouse button on the Ruler, then "Guidelines Setup"
  - ↳ or Tools/Options/Guidelines...

More on the Guidelines Menu follows next.

7.4.2 The Guidelines-Menu

By double clicking on a guideline you can open the menu divided into horizontal, vertical and all guidelines:

Guidelines visible or invisible

Line type and color for highlighted guidelines.

Choose Horizontal, Vertical or all guidelines to modify their settings.

Above you can specify precise coordinates, then use Add.
Or you can mark a guideline on crooked coordinates e.g. 20.143 and set 20 instead, and press Modify

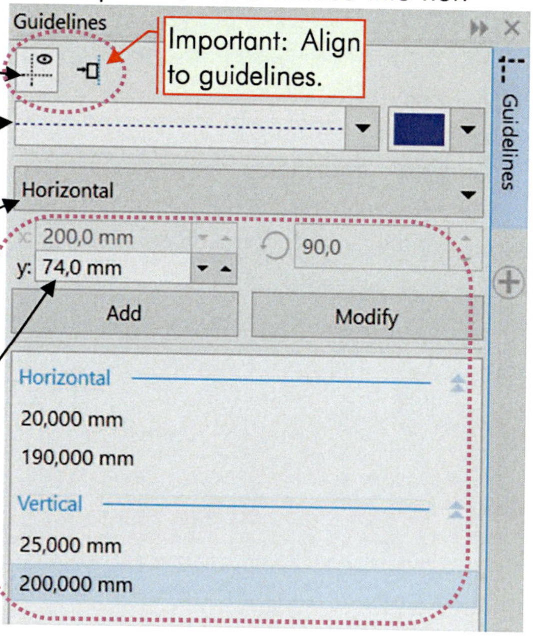

In the menu above you will find these symbols at the bottom:

Lock Guideline: Then the guidelines cannot be moved or deleted.

Delete the actual marked guideline (or with [Del] also.

7.4.3 Angled Guidelines-Menu

Switch in the Guidelines-Menu to the angled-guidelines. Here you can define angles for existing guidelines or set new guidelines in an angle:

Enter the coordinates and the angle, and you can set help lines with the exact desired angle (possible to move later in the drawing).

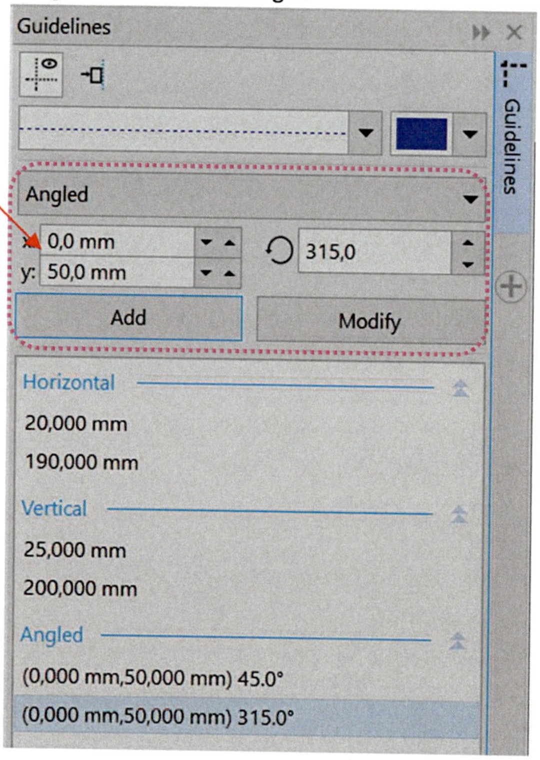

Also in the Property Bar you'll find symbols for the guidelines if one is marked (e.g. if marked by presets you'll find presets for one cm margins and more).

When you first set up the grid, guidelines are pulled into the drawing as desired.

7.5 Aligning On

The help lines are not used as long as the objects are not aligned with them.

[Ctrl]-Y

- With View you can switch on/off the visibility of the Grid or Guidelines.
- With View/Snap To you can switch on/off the snap function of the Grid or Guidelines.

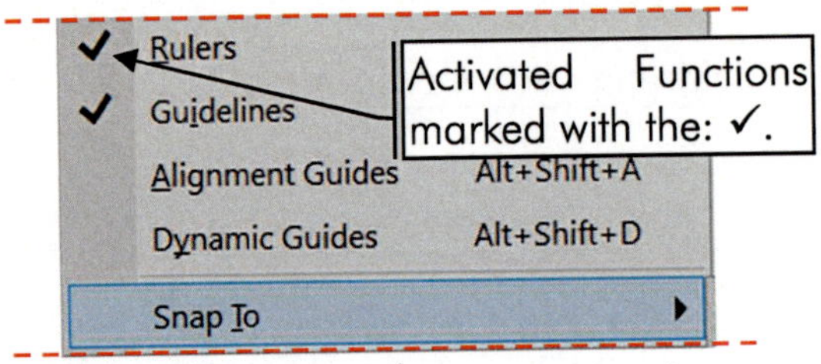

- Dynamic guidelines make constructing easier, since they appear automatically and indicate angles or references.

In the Property Bar you can directly set if a guideline is marked:

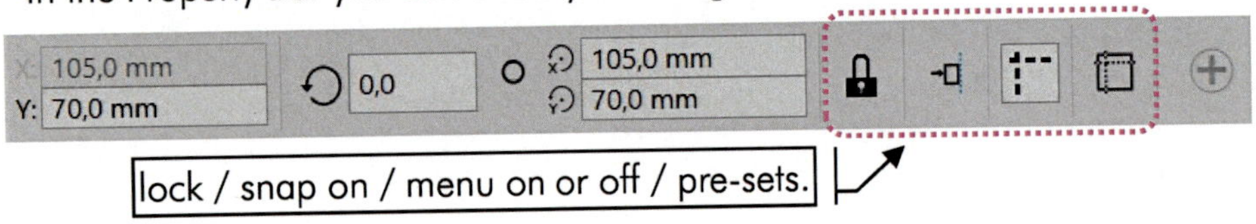

Use Snap On Grid **or** Snap on Guidelines; using both together sometimes has no effect!

7.6 Exercise: Truck

- ➢ Start a new drawing with DIN A5 crosswise and save as "Truck".
- ➢ Page setup: 6 x 3 meters and Grid each 0.2 m.
- ➢ Set below a horizontal line as the street.

So it should be:

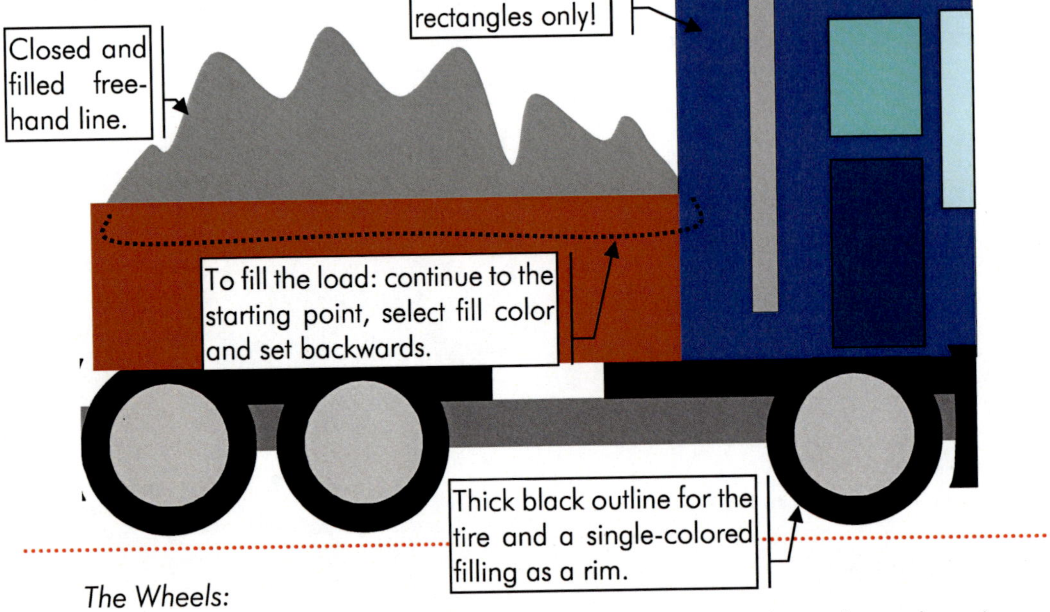

The Wheels:

- ➢ Draw the wheels as circles by pressing [Ctrl] or using the grid so it doesn't become a ellipse.
- ➢ Copy the first wheel twice. If you press [Shift] by copying you can move them exactly horizontally.

Chapter 8

8. Quadrates, Circles, Shapes

8.1 Quadrates and Circles

We have already created squares and circles by pressing the [Ctrl] key in the truck exercise before.

[Ctrl] = Circle, Quadrate; exact angle.

- By pressing [Ctrl]-Mouse Button you can draw
  - Lines in 15°-degree steps including 45°, 90° etc.
  - Instead of an ellipse, it will draw a circle and
  - instead of a rectangle, a quadrate.
- While pressing [Shift]-Mouse Button
  - a started ellipse, circle or rectangle will be drawn around the first point (the first point is the middle point and not the edge point as usual) or
  - you can change the size of objects around their middle point or
  - with [Ctrl]+[Shift] together you can draw a circle or quadrate around the first point.

[Shift]= around first point.

- Usage: This way, you can draw a circle exactly around a point or axis intersection point. If you click on this point and start drawing your object, you can press and hold [Ctrl]+[Shift] while drawing.

You do not have to remember this, just try it:

- Draw an ellipse or rectangle, but keep the left mouse button pressed and then try:
  - [Ctrl] or [Shift]-Button or both?
  - You'll see the effect on the screen as soon as you move the mouse slightly!

> Press and hold the left mouse button and try!
>
> If you want to move elements with the left mouse button pressed, or copy them with an additional right-click, it helps to touch the corner so that they remain on the grid points.

8.1.1 EXERCISE: QUADRATES AND CIRCLES WITH GUIDELINES AND GRID

- New Drawing with DIN A5 crosswise, save as "Quadrates and Circles".
- Draw for the exact horizontal arrangement with a guideline (and activate "Snap to Guidelines" first):

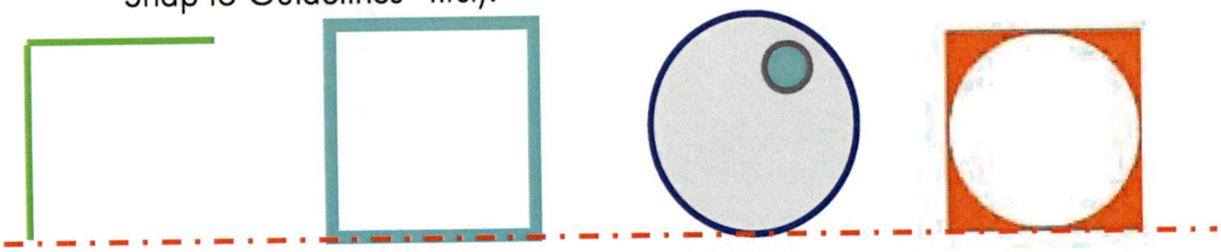

- For this new drawing use the grid marked every 10mm and draw one quadrate, then copy it with right mouse button. With one line or some quadrates ready, you can mark and copy multiple objects at once:

Now comes a very difficult but useful exercise:

- The differently colored filling is produced by copying the outer, largest circle several times inwards.
  - ↳ Hold down the [Shift] key so that the copied circles automatically get the same middle point.
- Fill each copied circle with the desired color.
  [Shift] = Reduce or enlarge around the center point.

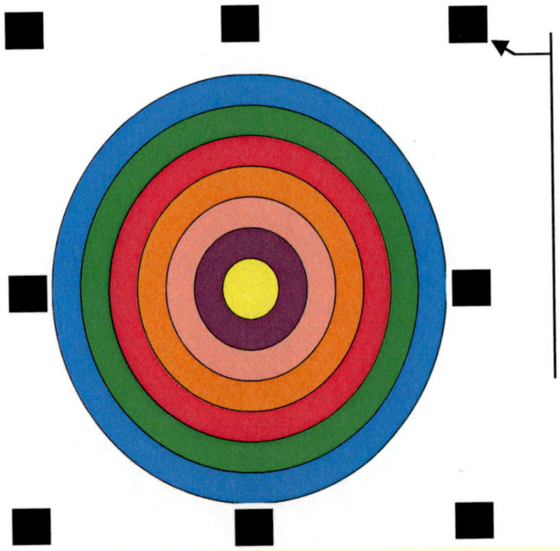

Draw the outer circle, then touch and reduce the touch point at the corner.
Click the right mouse button to initiate copying, and then hold the [Shift] key to decrease the center point.
Assign a different fill and line color to each new circle.

This is no problem if you press the right mouse button during the movement + holding down the left mouse button, then you can at any time try pressing [Shift] or [Ctrl] to find the target position.

8.2 Polygon, Spiral, Grinding

Corel also offers special shapes, which can be found with the polygon tool under the symbols for rectangles and circles. Draw the following:

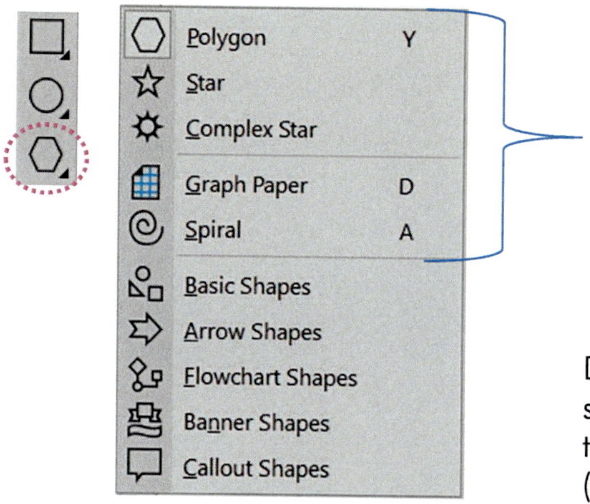

Draw first with the default, then you can set each of these elements by mouse or in the property bar. Thus, e.g. triangles (=three corners), octagons or stars:

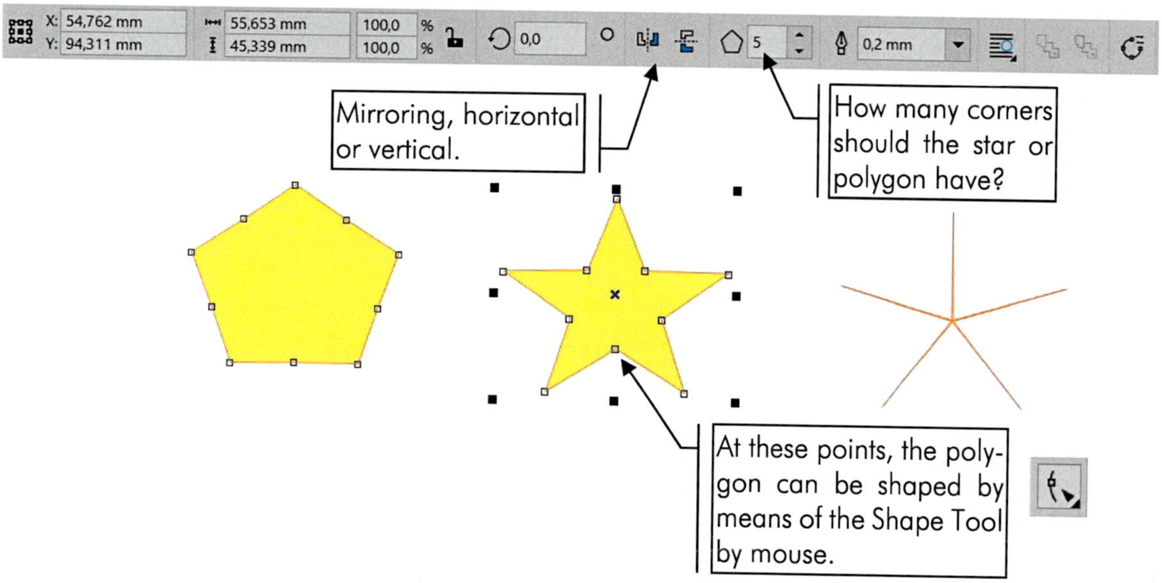

8.3 Preset Shapes (Basic, Arrow, Flowchart etc.)

Corel also has prefabricated standard shapes, e.g. for a flash, an arrow or various stars or speech bubbles.

➢ In the polygon menu, see above, you will find the shapes (Basic, Arrow Flowchart etc.), too. Select a form type, then you can select more in the property bar, here a sample for the Arrow Shapes:

Select a group in the Polygon menu, then the desired shape type in the property bar.

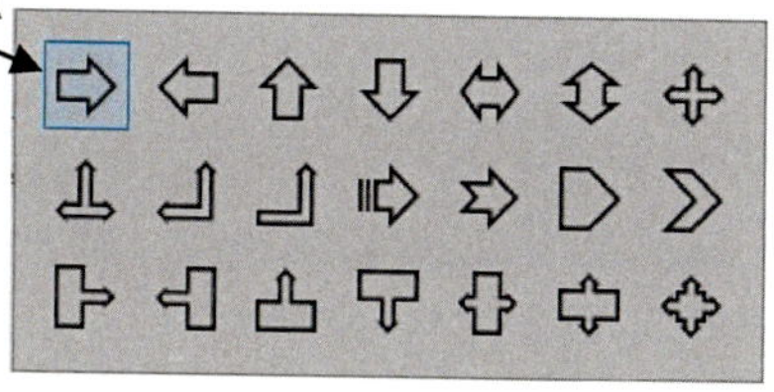

Of course, these shapes can also be retrofitted. Note the tap points.

Chapter 9

9. Lineal, Zero Point, Group

It is sometimes helpful to lay the zero point appropriately, for one wheel, for example, in the centre. Or to adjust the scale from the start instead, to manually count every dimension later.

9.1 Lineal and Zero Point

In order to specify the dimensions for a drawing, a Zero point is set and is scaled up horizontally (X-axis) and vertically (Y-axis).

(0, 0)

In a CorelDRAW Drawing you can read the coordinates on the rulers (at the top and left of the screen) and usually the zero point is the left bottom of the page, but depending on the drawing the zero point is sometimes better placed in the middle with 0 or lower right.

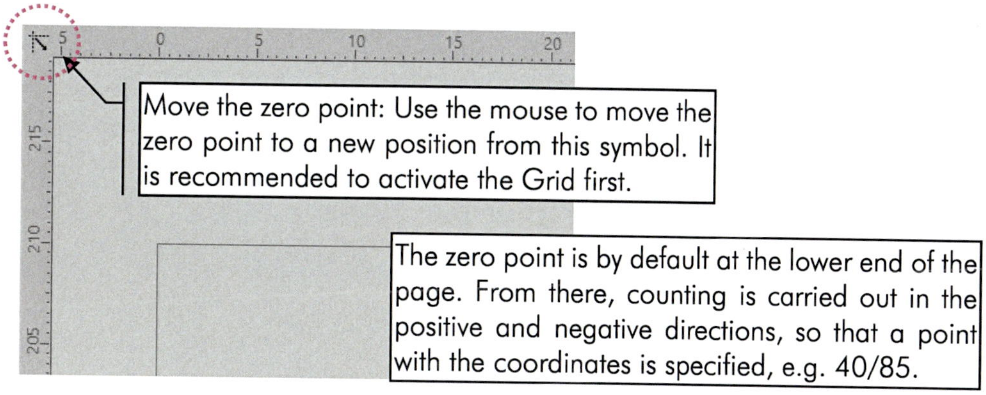

- Double-clicking on the ruler displays the settings menu.
  - In this menu, you could change the unit for the ruler to meters or inches, or specify the start position (0,0) at origin.
  - e.g. if you enter with a paper sized DIN A5 crosswise horizontal 210 is the zero point on the right side of paper.

If you click on the menu item "Edit Scale", a window appears, in which you can choose other scales:

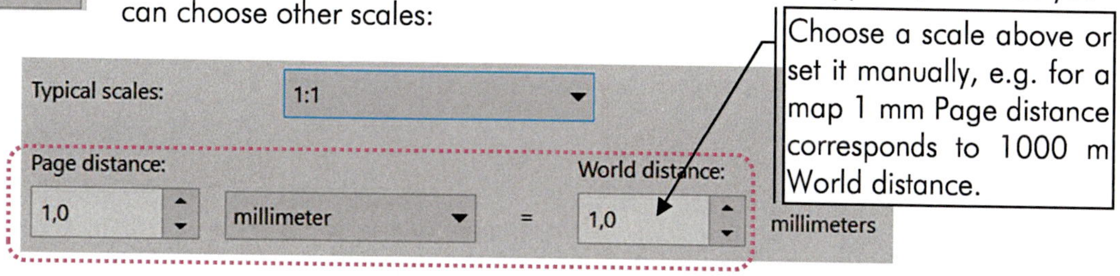

9.2 EXERCISE: RAILWAY WHEEL

We want to draw a railway wheel. Preparations:

- Start a new drawing, choose centimeters as the units and set the size to 100x100 cm:

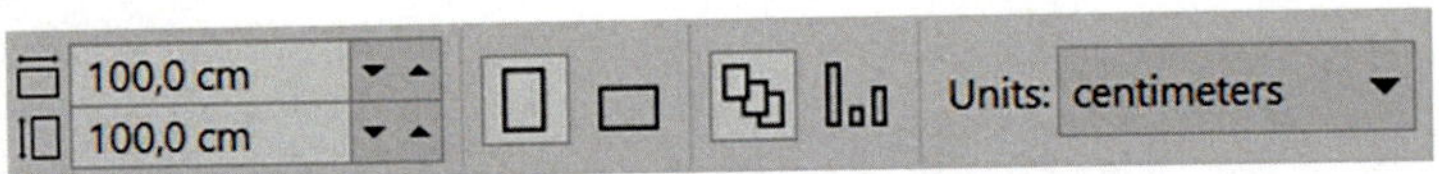

- Double-click on the ruler and set the origin at 50, 50 cm so that it is exactly in the center of the page.
  - ↳ Then, use the Zoom Tool to select "Whole Page" to see the result.
- Place the grid every 5 cm (centimeters apart) and turn on the grid and guidelines.

> Attention! Corel only points at the grid points when you click or release near a point!

- Set a horizontal Guideline at 0 and a vertical at 0 because the origin 0/0 is now in the center of the page.

Drawing is easier now with the guidelines and grid:

- Draw a large circle: Set the starting point exactly in the middle, then draw the circle while pressing [Ctrl]+[Shift]-Button around this middle point.
- We cannot simply draw the smaller circle, since we could move the first circle. Therefore, we copy the first circle and reduce it:
  - ↳ Touch and hold down the corner handles, right-click for copying, press [Shift], locate the target position and release the mouse.
  - ↳ Mark both circles, then **combine** them and choose a filling color.

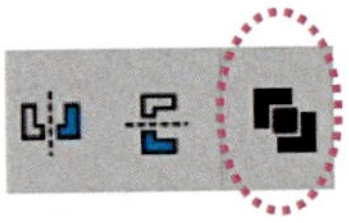

- Just as the small axis circles can be drawn, combining would not be necessary here since both circles can be filled simply in color if the smaller circle is at the front.
- Now draw the first horizontal spoke and place it at the back. If necessary, switch off the grid using [Ctrl]-Y.

The first spoke is copied while rotating:

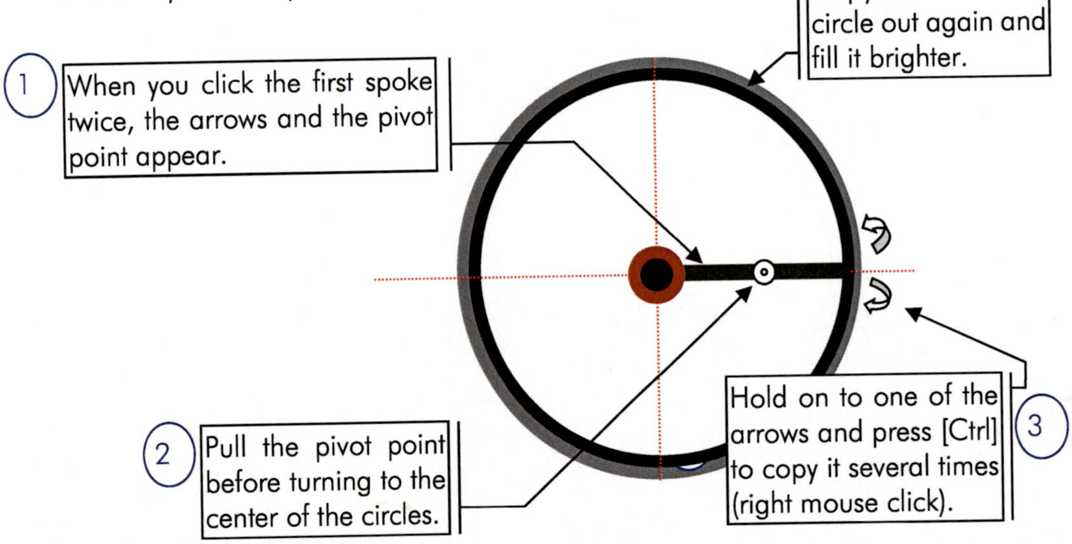

9.3 The Menu "Transformations"

Actions with the mouse go quickly, but those elements can be inadvertently moved just as quickly. If you want to be more precise, you can use the Transformation Menu (Object/Transformations/...).

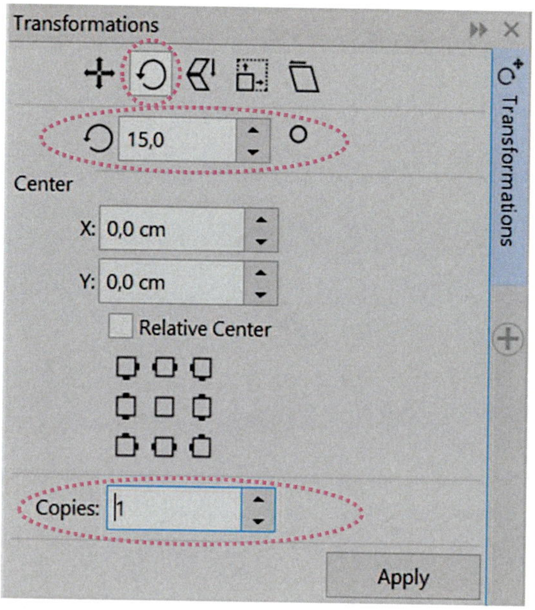

You can use the different map types to perform all actions as with the mouse, except that you enter exact coordinates here. This offers two advantages:

- It is more comfortable and you can undo all actions here, even after you have executed numerous other commands.
  An example:
  - It can be drawn without accidentally moving a background - it can temporarily be moved by 300 mm to the side edge - when everything is done, the background is reset by -300 mm.

Perfectly draw the railway wheel:

- Use the Undo to erase the rotated spokes from the exercise using the mouse, then rotate the first spoke (the center of rotation is already in the center of the wheel) with Object/Transformation/Rotate.
  - If the angle of rotation does not fit evenly, reverse and try again with a different angle.

Add rivets:

The rotation works so well that we can rotate same way some rivets

- Draw with a high zoom one rivet as a radial filled circle.

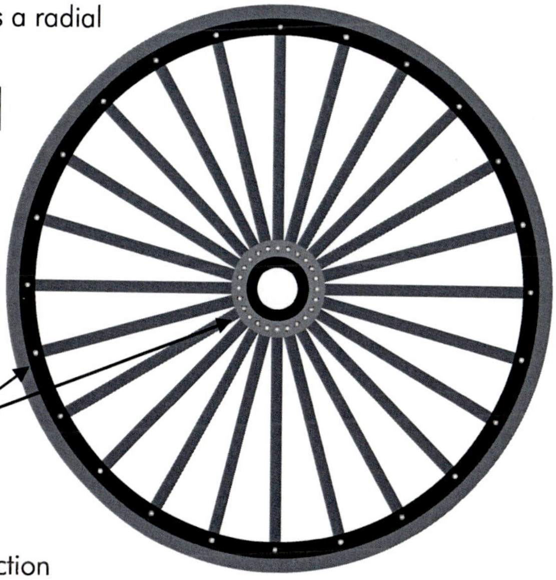

- Move the rotation point in the middle and copy around the wheel:

Draw one rivet as a radial filled circle and copy it the same way as the spokes with Object-Transformation around the wheel.

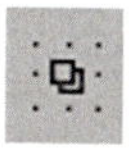

- Afterwards, mark all with a big selection frame or [Ctrl]-A and Group Objects.
- **Save** as "railway wheel" because we'll need it later to copy into our drawing of the train.

9.4 Group Objects

Complex drawings are not a problem if they are divided into small groups. As soon as a wheel is finished, for example, this can be grouped into one element and can then be duplicated as often as required.

Advantages of Grouping:

- Easy to copy or move because only one object needs to be selected.
- There is no more danger of inadvertently moving or deleting a small part like a rivet while you continue tracing.

Different ways of Grouping:

- You can group by symbol in the property bar (far right), in the menu (Object/Group…) or with the shortcut [Ctrl]-G.

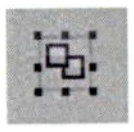

  - ↳ Grouping is only possible if several elements have been selected.
  - ↳ If "Ungroup" is active instead of Grouping, the group has already been grouped.

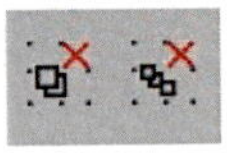

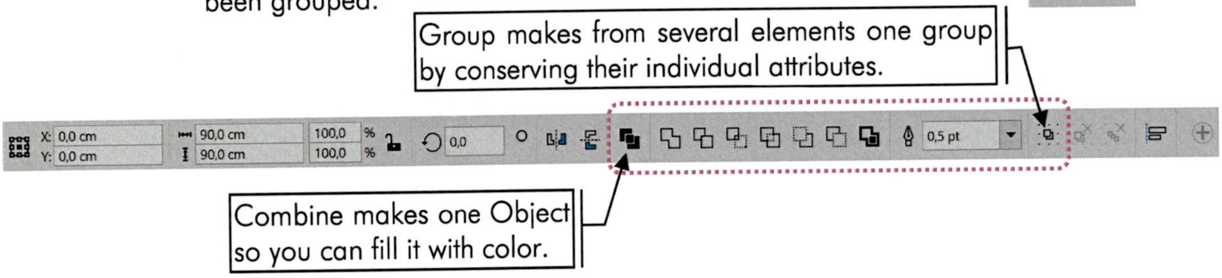

If you want to edit an element of a group again:

- While holding down the [Ctrl] key, single elements can be selected from a group and edited individually.
  - ↳ For example, to assign a different color, you must release the [Ctrl] key to pick the color.
- Or you could un-group, edit items as usual, and then re-group them. The latter is recommended for extensive modifications.

9.4.1 Exercise: Blossom

We'll do a similar exercise to the railway wheel, but this one may be easier.

- ➢ We want to draw a blossom: draw a circle in the middle and one ellipse as the first petal.
- ➢ Rotate the ellipse like petals around the flower. Before turning, push the center of rotation into the middle.
- ➢ Then, mark and group everything with a large selection frame or [Ctrl]-A.
- ➢ While holding down the [Ctrl] key, select individual petals from the group and change the color.

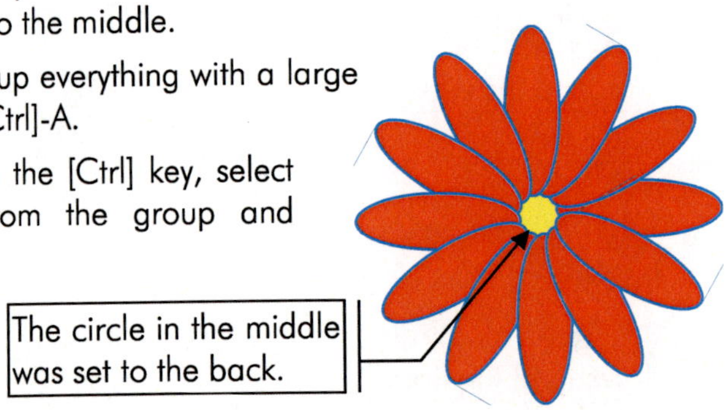

Chapter
10

10. Text and Symbols

10.1 Text Editing in Corel

➢ Start a new drawing A4 crosswise, then choose the text-editing tool (A).

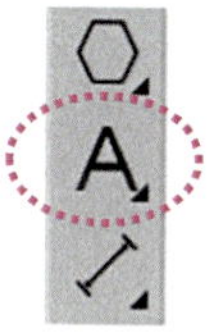

Now you have to tell the computer where you want to place the text., because we are using a drawing program, not a text program, and can put the text anywhere.

➢ Click on the desired location in the drawing and write: "Sample Text"

➢ Copy this sample text sometimes as training material. You can copy text similar to other objects this way:

  ★ Use the Pick Tool to move, and then copy it multiple times using the right mouse button.

10.1.1 Text Formatting with the Property Bar

The easiest way to format the text, as in a word processor, is with the Property Bar.

➢ When you click a text, you will find these icons for text formatting in the feature bar:

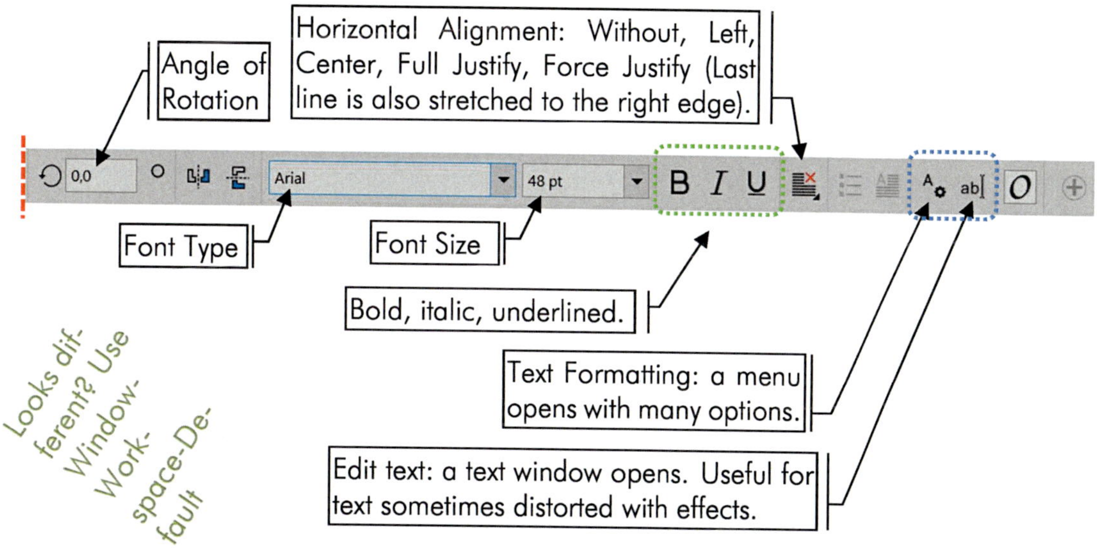

Looks different? Use Window-Workspace-Default

♦ Select what you want to adjust:

  ↳ by pressing the [Shift] key with the Pick Tool,

  ↳ Or by pressing the left mouse button within a text with the Text Tool.

10.1.2 Modify Text with the Pick Tool

When you finish the text editing, the text is an object like a rectangle or line, so you can edit the text as well:

- Click on the text with the Pick Tool once:
  - ↳ to change the text size at the Handle Points or
  - ↳ to catch the text and move it to another position (try to click on the text body, not on a handle point) or
  - ↳ Click while moving the right mouse button for copying.
- Click on the text with the Pick Tool a second time and you can:

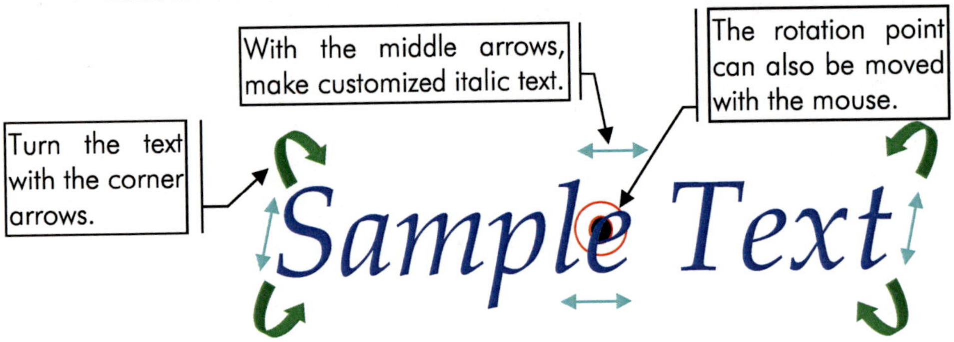

That's how it should be:

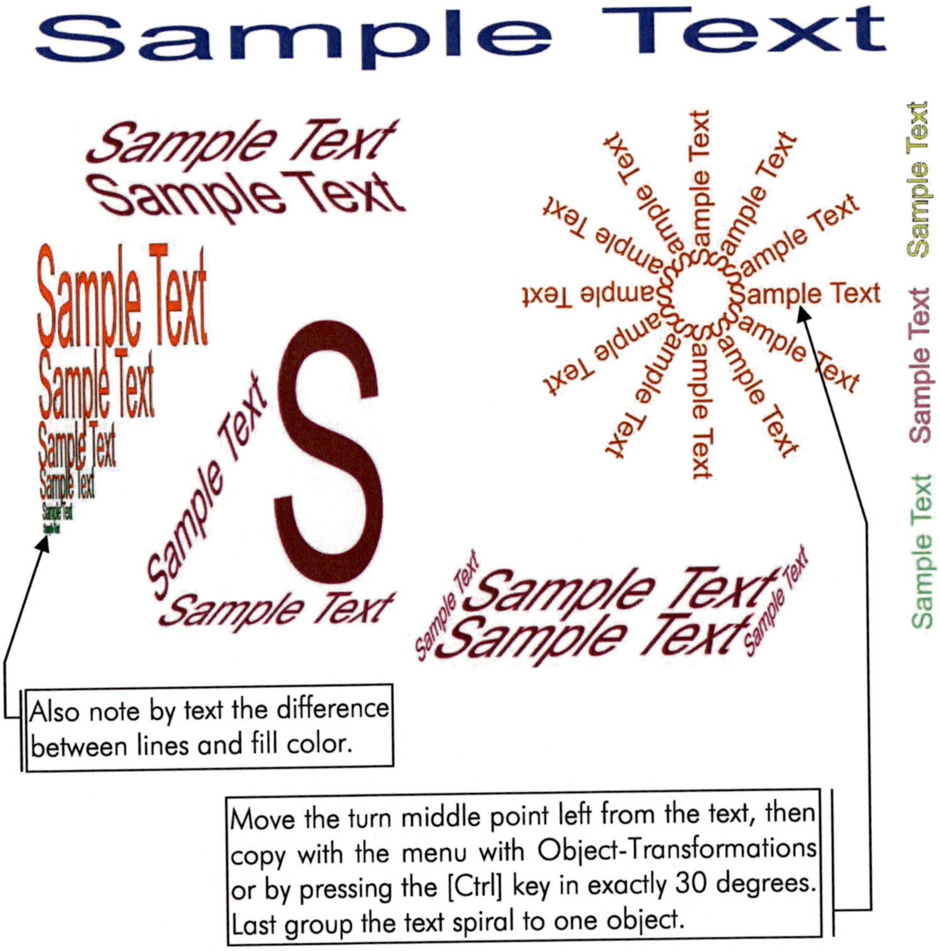

Double clicking on text switches to the Text Tool!

10.2 Exercise: Solar

To complete the basics for drawing, let's try an exercise with lines, a circle and text. Draw the following letterhead before setting up grids and guide lines:

Preparation:

- New Drawing, *set page with* 80mm width and 50mm height, set Grid suitable, two Guidelines and activate Snap On.

Circle and Lines:

- Draw the Circle ([Ctrl] key) for the sun with yellow filling and line.
- Draw the first vertical line:
  - Click two times on this line (not a double-click) and move the center point to the center of the sun.
  - Now you can copy each turn with right mouse button click and press the [Ctrl] key on the lines each 15°.
- Draw the rectangle for the solar module and rotate and arrange it appropriately to shorten the solar beams.

Corner Rounding:

- For the rounding of the corners, you can find these controls in the Properties bar:

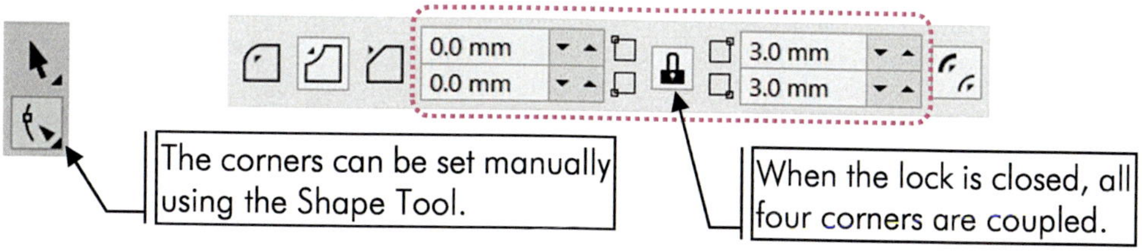

- Write the text and format it centered, place two rectangles as a background and fill it appropriately (draw a rectangle, then copy it down and change the fill color).
  - Use the grid or the coordinate fields in the property bar to set the rectangles to exact coordinates so you can place the text perfectly in the middle of it.

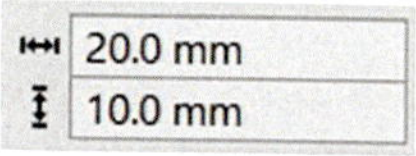

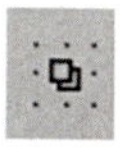

- Mark all with [Ctrl]-A or a big mark rectangle and group it – so it is useable as letterhead. .

  - Copy it into your word processing program as letterhead in the header. You can export in CorelDRAW as a wmf file for the best compatibility with MS Office programs.

10.3 The Symbol Fonts

The content of Windows and the Corel program package are special fonts that contain pictures instead of letters. Of these fonts only examples were installed on your computer, as installed fonts occupy memory.

- New exercise: the menu for symbol fonts can be opened with [Ctrl]-[F11] or Text/Insert Character.

On the right side, a docker appears:

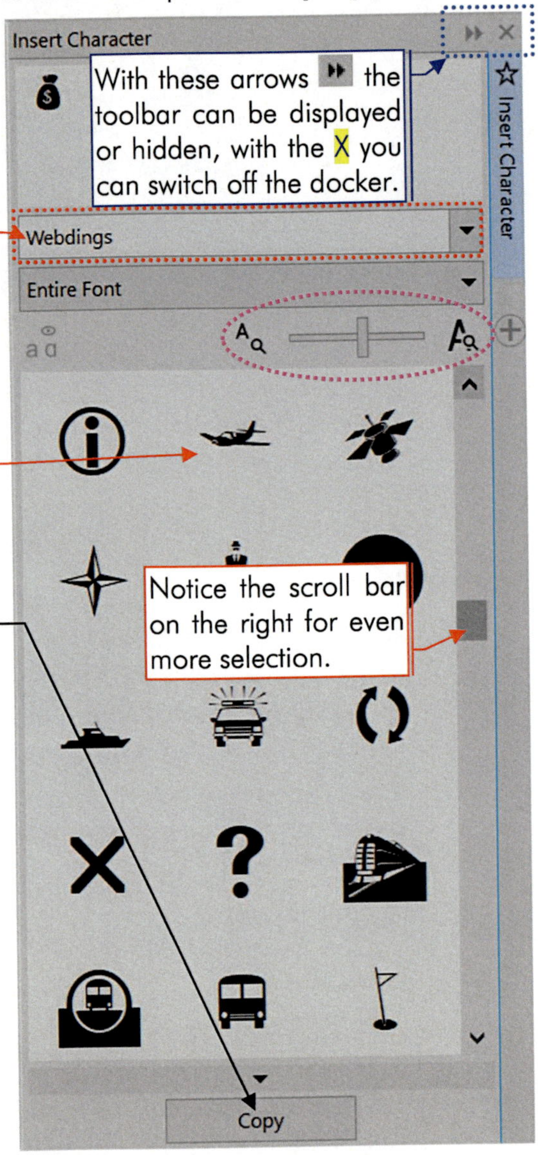

Choose the font here.
It is recommended to browse through the pages for the first time to check which fonts are available (note Webdings and Wingdings),

then pull the desired symbol with the mouse into the drawing

or click on the symbol, copy it and then click with the Text Tool in the drawing – you can choose a position in an existing text, too – and insert.

Interesting fonts: Yu Gothic and MS Reference Speciality with fractions and special characters, Wingdings, Webdings, Symbol, fonts with Chinese characters: MingLiU and MS JhengHei.

Integrate a symbol into a text:

These special characters can also be inserted into a text from this Corel menu: if the text is opened with the text tool (cursor flashes at the desired location), double-click on the character you want to insert.

Then, the special character is inserted into the text, consequently just as a normal letter moves and changes e.g. with the font size.

Only the font can't be changed afterwards because the new font also applies to the special character. If it is necessary to change the font type of the text, then reinsert the symbol or reassign the character font to the symbol.

After inserting the object correctly with the Shape Tool the letter distance should match

Third Part

Colors

Fillings, ClipArt, Photos

Chapter 11

11. Single Fillings

11.1 Overview select Filling and adjust

- You can choose colors from the color palette:
  - ✎ Select the object and change the fill color with the left mouse button, and the line color with the right one.
- For more precise color selection or special color fillings, there are two symbols in the Tool Bar:

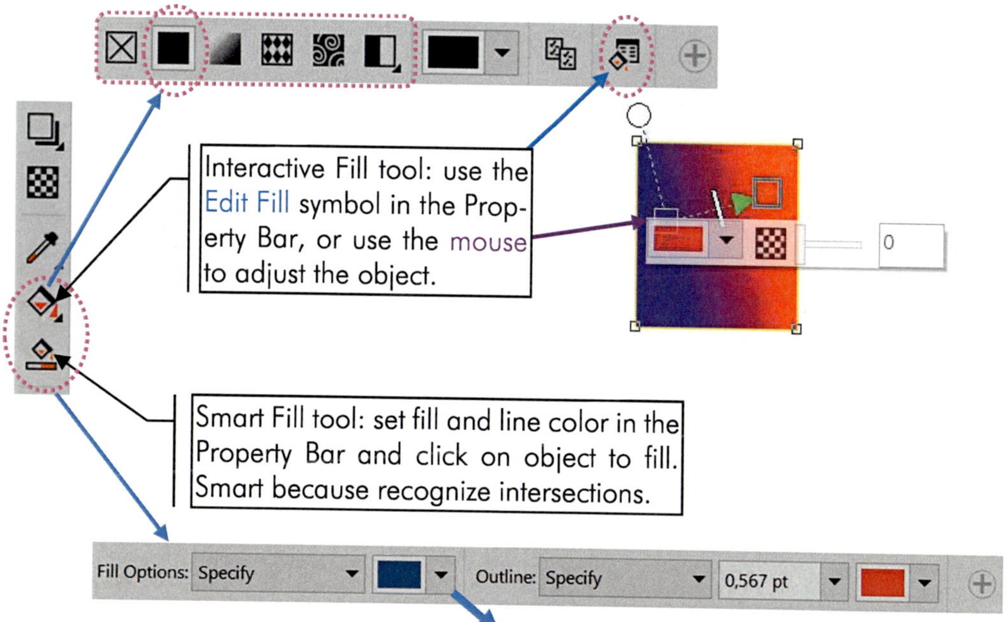

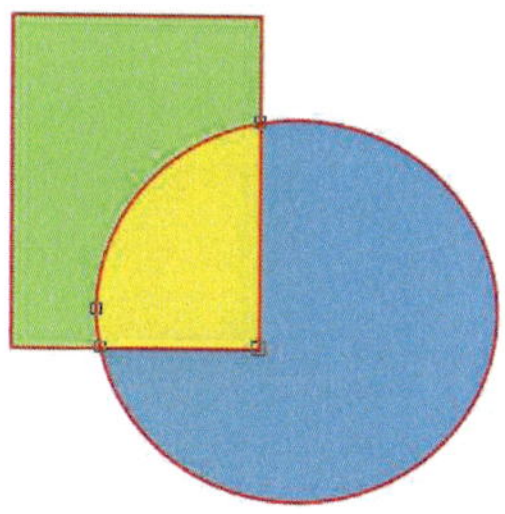

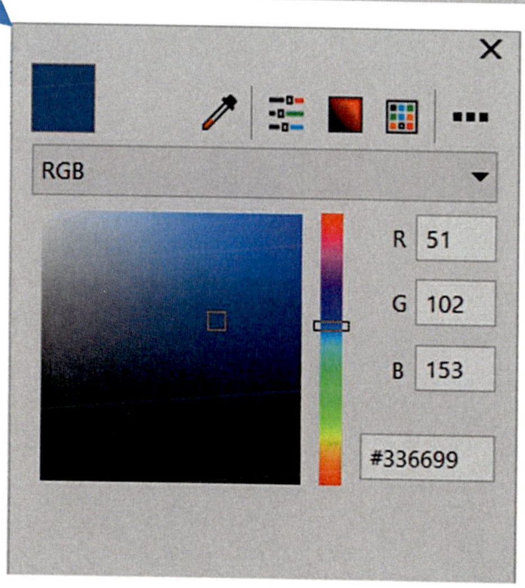

A detailed description of both methods follows. Which method you use is personal taste.

11.2 Modify the Preset

Before we set colors, a little hint. If nothing is selected, Corel assumes that you want to change the general preferences. Two examples to illustrate this:

- If nothing is selected and you click a color, you could set this color as the default for all new objects.
- If nothing is selected and you select a line thickness from the line menu (pencil symbol), all lines will be drawn with this thickness in the future.
- This can be arbitrarily extended, e.g. If you select a different font without a text selected, you could save this font as a default.

Therefore, for each action: if nothing is selected, you change the default setting if you confirm the appearing warning window with OK:

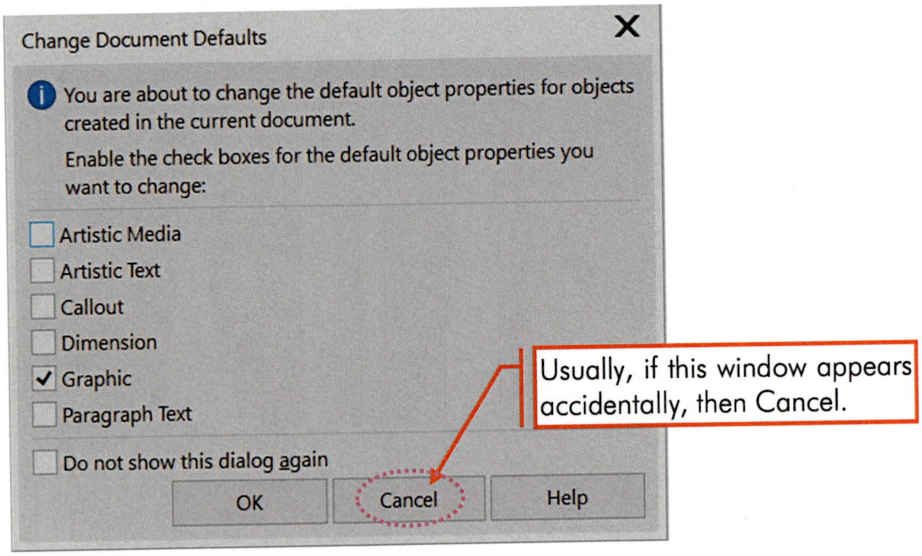

- If you change the default settings with OK, this applies only to the current drawing.
- By Tools/Save Settings as Default you can also save the presets for all new drawings.

> You cannot undo this. You can only reset it by the reverse process, e.g. select without something marked to make the line color black, or no fill color.

11.3 The Color Palette

- Open the Pyramid Squares exercise so you can try something out.
- Open some more color palettes by Window/Color Palettes.
- Close all open palettes but not the Default palette. You can close unmark by Window/Color Palettes or by this arrow at top of the pallet:

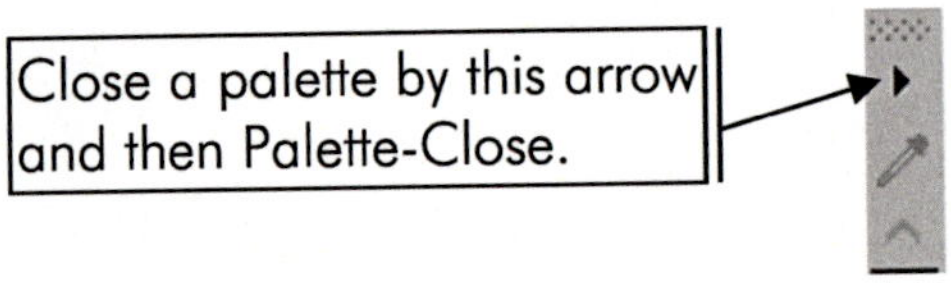

If you want to select many colors, it is convenient to drag the color palette into the center of the drawing.

So colors can choose easy:

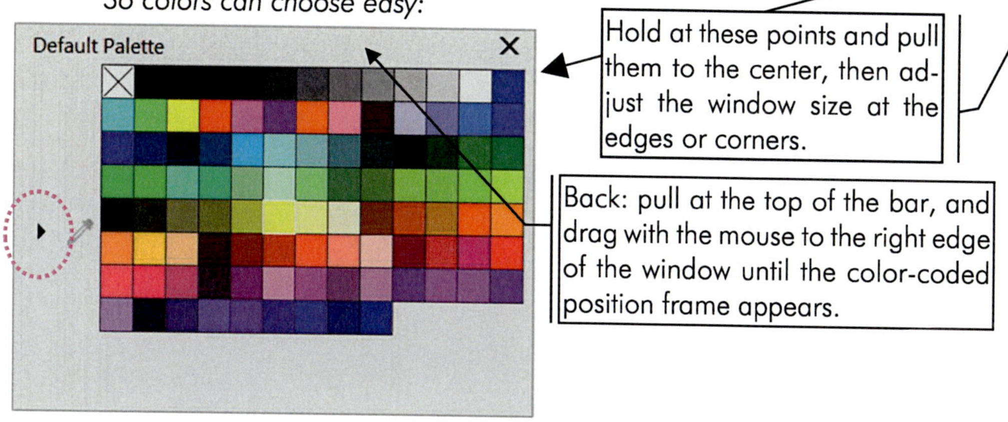

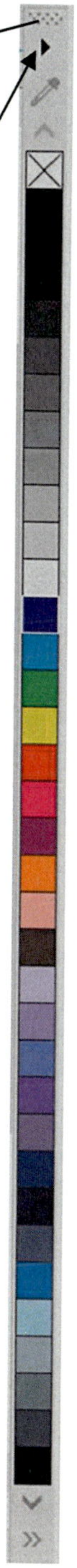

- You can switch to a different color palette by Window/Color Palette, which is automatically positioned right again.
  - ➪ By Window/Color Palette you can switch off color palettes.

Instead of using the palettes, you can also adjust each color manually.

11.4 Color Settings

The complete fill menu can be found like this:

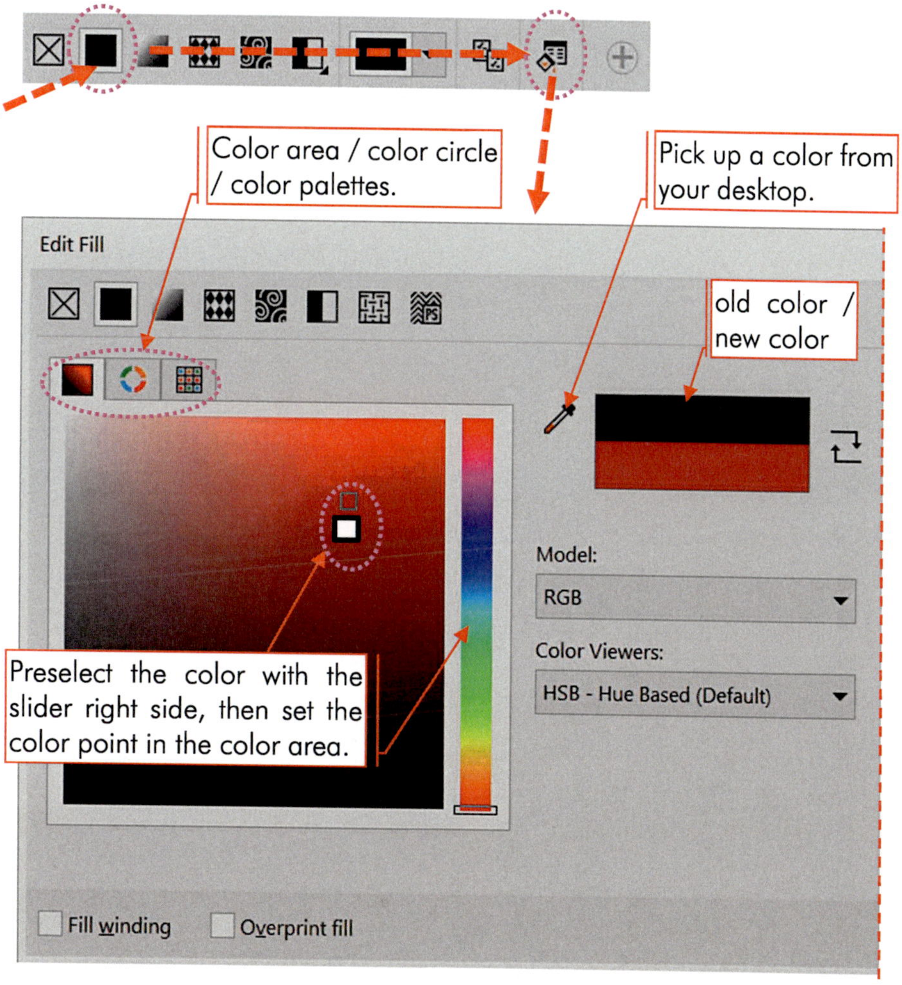

11.5 Color Circle and Color Models

In this menu you can switch to the color circle, another way to choose a color:

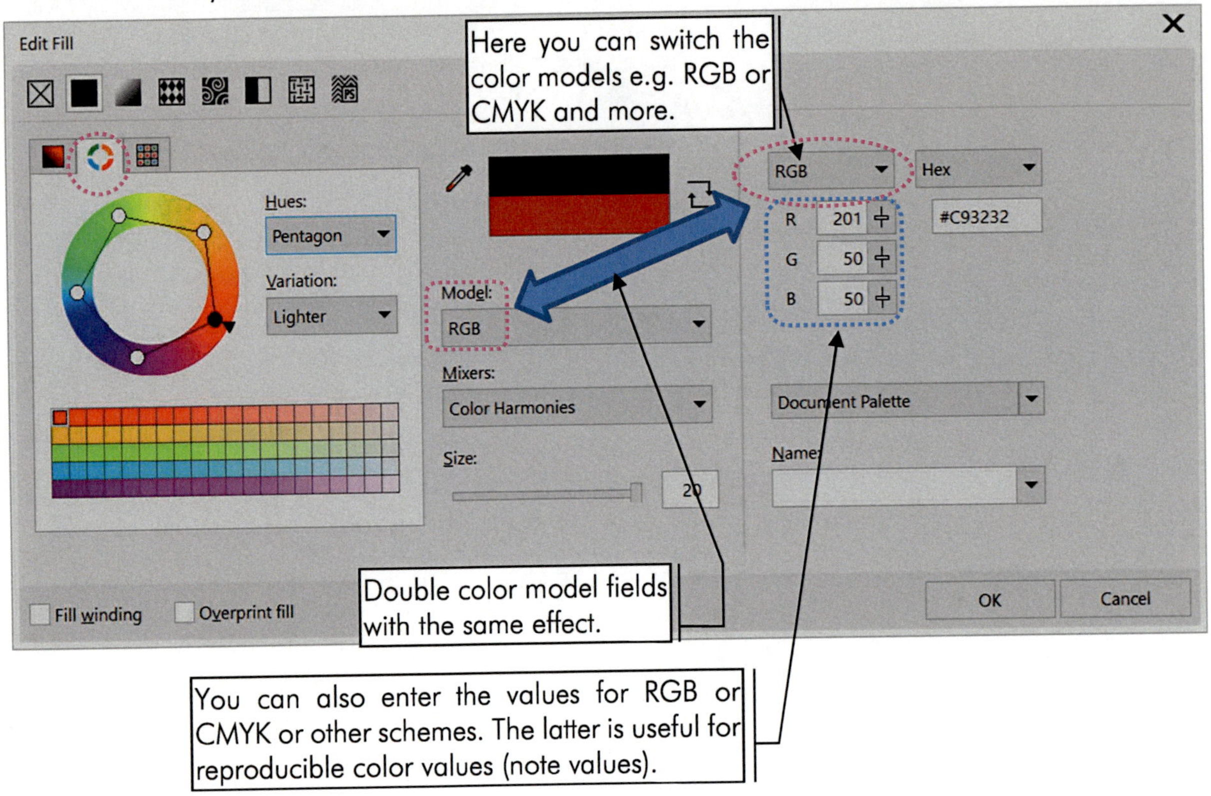

Important Color Models:

- CMYK: the color model used by offset printing and every four color printer. It means: C=CYAN, M=MAGENTA, Y=YELLOW, K=BLACK.
- RGB is the color sheme of every monitor and TV. All colors are mixed from the base colors RED, GREEN and BLUE.
  - ↳ RGB is a so named additive color scheme, because all colors together result in white (light is mixed), while by CMYK all colors together result in black, all colors off in white (= subtractive scheme).

11.6 Color Palettes

CorelDRAW has some color palettes. Switch to the palettes in the previous menu:

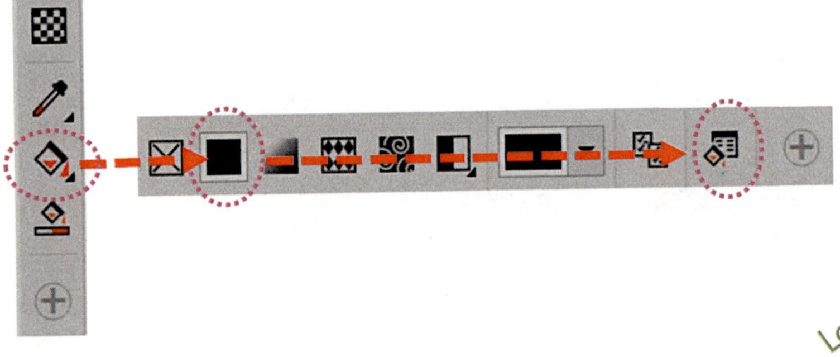

Looks different? Use Window-Workspace-Default

The Color Palettes:

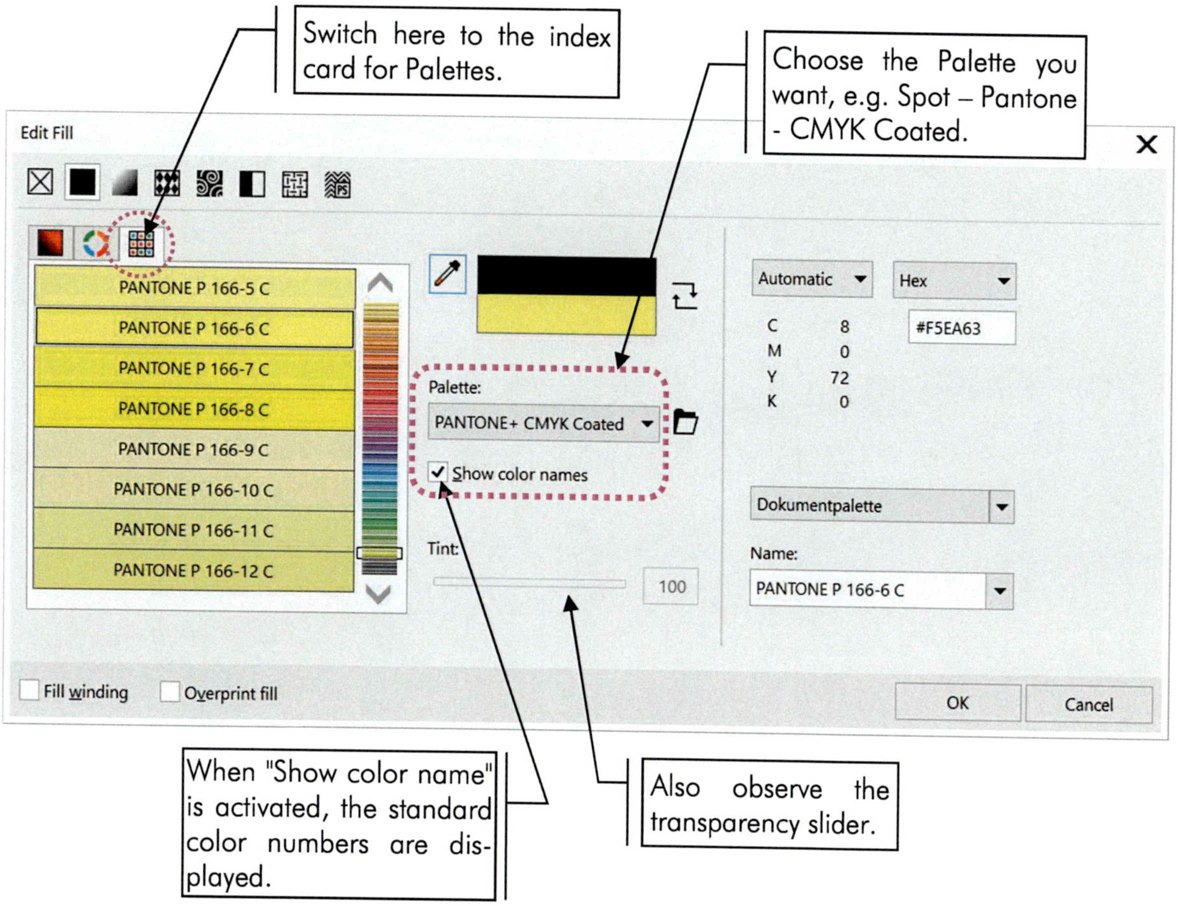

About the Palettes:

- Palettes are standardized color palettes used by painters and printers, so that colors can be accurately reproduced, e.g.:
- Colors according to the Focoltone, a scheme you use when you paint your rawhide wallpaper.
- Pantone colors are the standard in graphics and printing, and are also used for interior decoration, cosmetics and product design.
- With Window/Color Palettes/Color Palettes Manager a clear window with the color palettes is opened. Here you could also create your own palette.

The palettes are very important when a color needs to be exactly reproduced:

- If you change the painter or the printing company, the stationery letterhead or the business card can be printed again in exactly the same colors.
  - If you use the palette colors in Corel and specify the numbers to the printer, the colors fit as planned.
  - It is ideal if you use a printed color palette catalogue because your monitor and printer don't show the colors exactly the same.

> The use of the color palettes allows identical colors on business cards, letterheads, company signs, painting, etc.

Chapter

12

12. Fountain Fill

Color Gradient Fillings are nice and versatile.

➢ Open the exercise "Pyramids Squares" (s. P. 50) and choose the "Interactive Fill Tool".

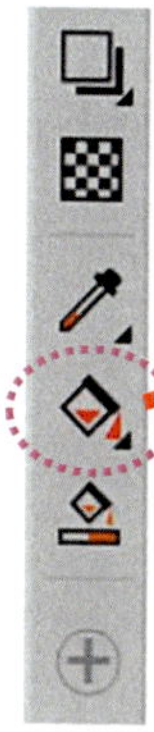

Now we choose the next option, "Fountain Fill":

- X = shut off filling
- Monochrome filling
- Fountain Fill, e.g. color transition from orange to green,
- Vector pattern fill: Brick wall, chessboard, coins, stones…
- Bitmap pattern fill: Cherries, tablets, peanuts…
- Two color pattern fill: easy fillings with only two colors,
- PostScript fill.

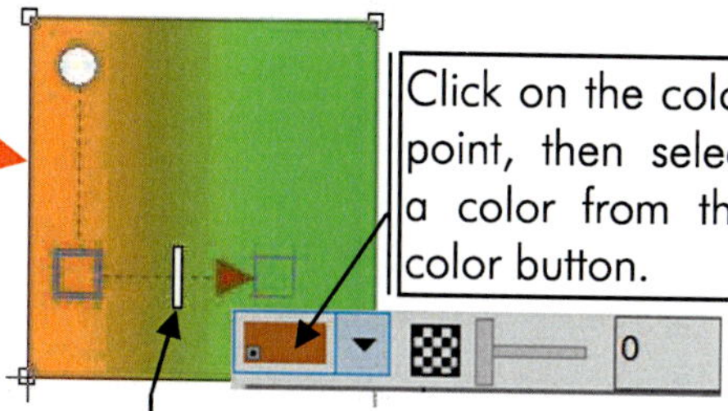

Click on the color point, then select a color from the color button.

Use the slider to move the color center point.

In these next exercises, you can try various filling types in each square:

Text can fill, too.

12.1 ADJUST THE FOUNTAIN FILL

You can change a fill at any time. Let's try it. The fountain fill should be at the -37° angle.

- ➢ Choose the Interactive Fill Tool, then click on a new rectangle and edit the fill in the property bar on the right-most symbol:

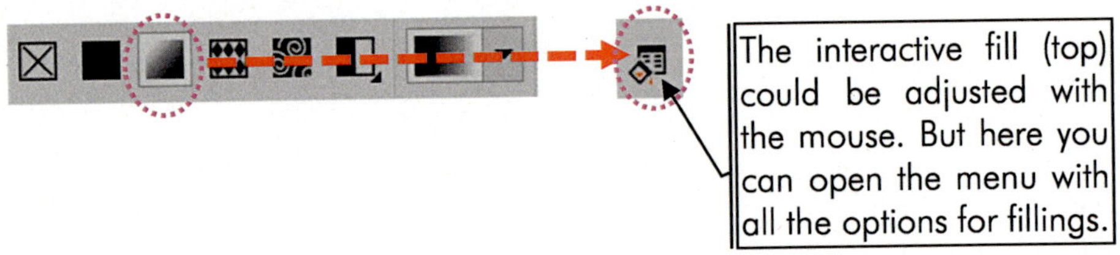

Here in the menu you can easily set up the filling:

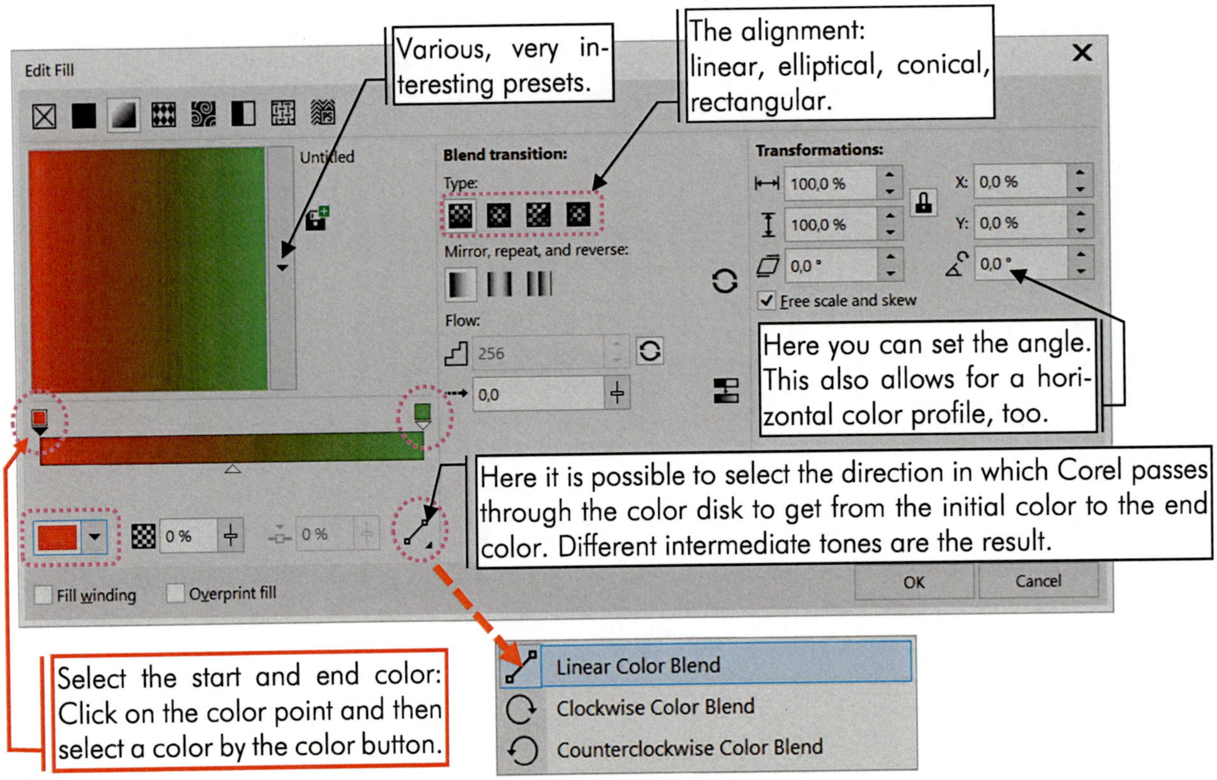

The alignment:

linear:	elliptical:	conical	rectangular:
			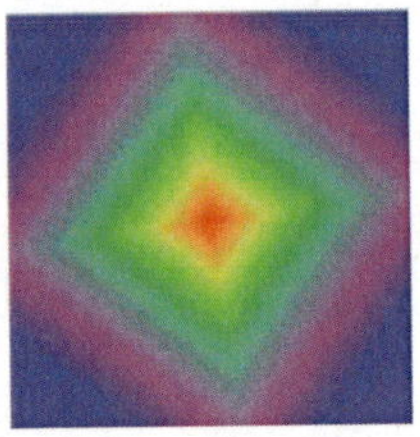

- ➢ Try different fountain fillings and set them to some squares of the exercise.

12.2 Multiple Color Filling

With these settings for the color profile, a two-color or multi-color filling can also be achieved.

Set up the color gradient filling:

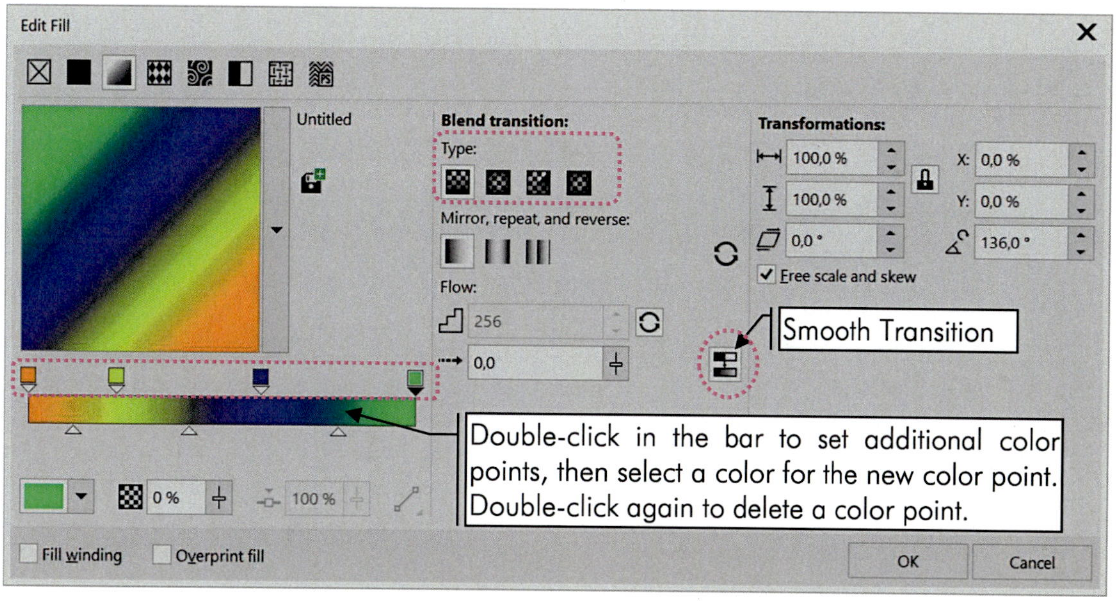

- The initial and final colors can also be selected on the square boxes at the left and right end of the bar.
- Any number of additional color points can be set. For each point a color can be determined.
- Color points can be moved with the mouse.

The preset 256 color streaks cause smooth transitions, since the fine stripes are not visible. Multi-strips cause unnecessary computational overhead, but sometimes it is desirable to deliberately reduce the number of strips so that the individual color strips become visible.

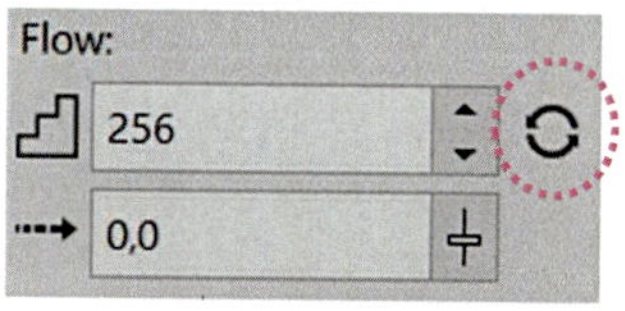

- To change the number of strips, first click the icon next to it (the rotating arrows). Then try to reduce it from 256 to e.g. 3, 4, 5.
- By Transformations, the size of the color gradient can be set, at 80% the 20% at the edge remains with the start and end color.

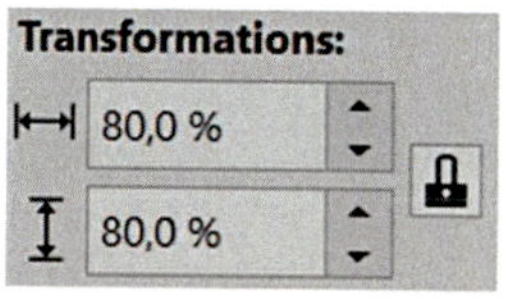

- If you have a border area in this area:
  - ↳ Default: the start and end color
  - ↳ Mirror & repeat: the fountain fill starts again, mirrored.
  - ↳ Reverse: the fountain fill starts again from the start to end color.

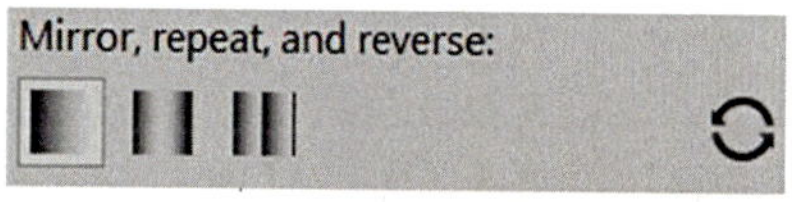

In the border area the filling is repeated. So this is only visible if you have a border area with Transformation less than 100% or if you use an elliptical or conical filling (there, you have a border area in the edges of the filled rectangle).

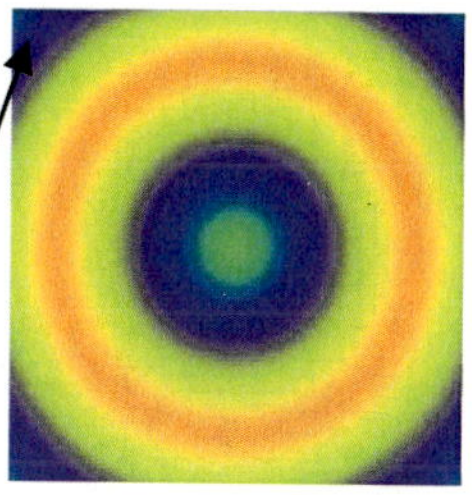

12.3 EXERCISE: CHRISTMAS CARD

An easy exercise with many color gradient fillings:

- Use the format Envelope C5 crosswise:

Draw a tree with the polyline (by pen):

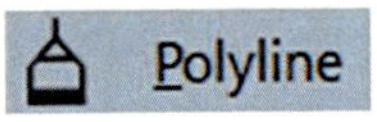

- With the Polyline, click once for the next line, Double-Click to stop. Draw roughly from the end to the starting point.
- Then, choose the Shape Tool and correctly move the points until it becomes like a Christmas tree.
- Finally, set a green fill.

The tree trunk and the jewelry:

- Paint the trunk (freehand line) with a brown filling, then set backwards - so you can draw the trunk higher and so the section does not match exactly.
- Finally draw the jewelry as filled circles once, then copy several times. Ideal: radial or rectangular color filling or a preset.

Freehand Line: double-click draws further, one click stops. Polyline: single click draws further, double-click stops.

Group and duplicate the Christmas tree:

- Mark the tree with a bigger mark rectangle using the Pick Tool and group it (with symbol or Object/Group).
  - ✎ Now as a group you can easily copy the tree by clicking the right mouse button while moving it to another side.

The Gifts:

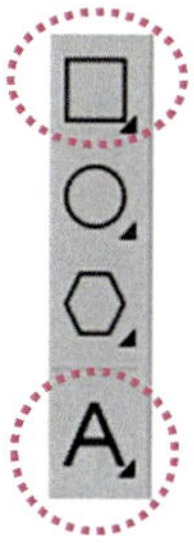

- Draw the gifts, each with a different fill and line color as filled rectangles.
- Place the gifts forward or backward accordingly. Finally, group the gifts.
- We have used a basic form. It would be nicer if you searched in Corel Connect or the web for a clipart.

Text and background:

- Write the Text as usual with the Text tool and move it to the right position with the mouse. For an exact position you can use the coordinate fields in the Property bar,
- Set a rectangle with fountain fill and rounded edges behind the text on the top,
- Use the Polygon tool and find the Banner shapes.
- Use it to draw a big rectangle with same dimensions as the paper, set it in the background, and format it with a fountain fill.

12.4 Exercise: Carton home

Create a template for a door sign.

Prepare drawing:

- New file, page format DIN A5 high. Set a grid width of 5mm and align to grid, but not yet to guidelines, since this is predominant and is no longer aligned with the grid when we start near a guideline.
- Set guidelines as edge boundaries.

Copy the rectangles:

- Draw the first rectangle and adjust it in size.

- Complete the first row by copying. If necessary, delete it again and change the size of the first rectangle.

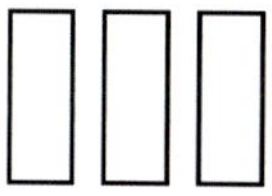

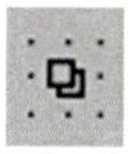

- Make a group out of the first line, then copy this line twice downward.
- Make a group of the first block again and copy a second time downward right.

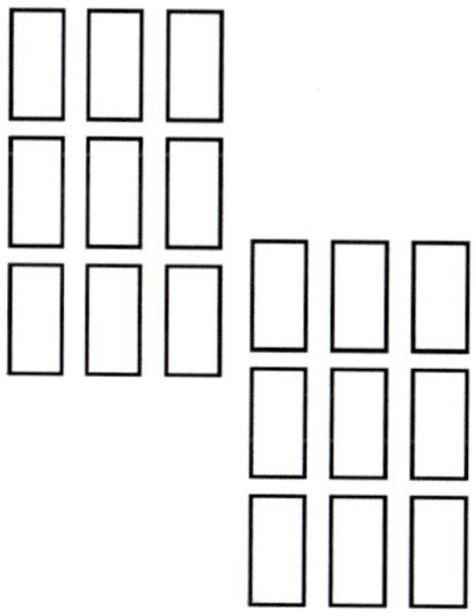

- Mark all and set a matching fountain fill with an angle.
  - ↳ Aslant fountain fills are very nice most of the time but the direction should be not right down, but top right.
- Complete the text, write "Carton-", click elsewhere, and write "home", click on another place and write "Manufacture".

- Now you can set these three graphic texts to the guideline on the left side and expand to the guideline on the right side. At last, expand it above to set the height.

  ↳ If finished, mark the text and set a matching fountain fill.

- Complete it with the address block left bottom. Copy the filling.
- Mark all text and add a Drop Shadow and choose in the Property bar the preset Medium Glow. In the Property bar you can choose a nice color for the shadow:

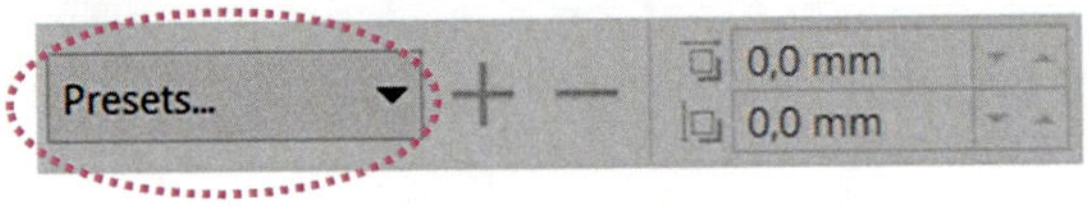

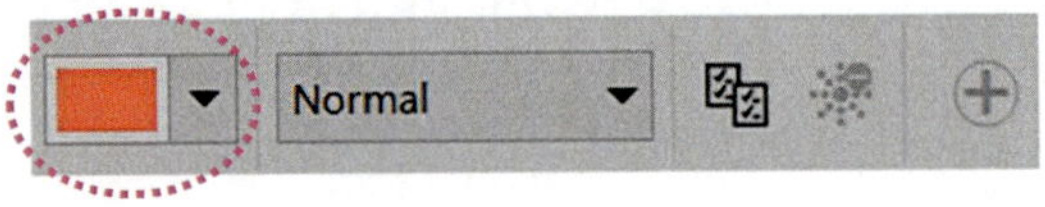

- Finish the exercise with a rectangle the same size as the paper and a fountain fill as the background. Here we use a conical-reverse fountain fill:

12.5 Exercise: Steam Locomotive

This drawing is already challenging in a course with support, but it is a good exercise that shows that it is not so difficult to create complex drawings.

- New file, switch the units to meters and then set 30 meters long and 10 meters high. Display the whole page and set the grid to 0.2m each and activate "Snap on grid".

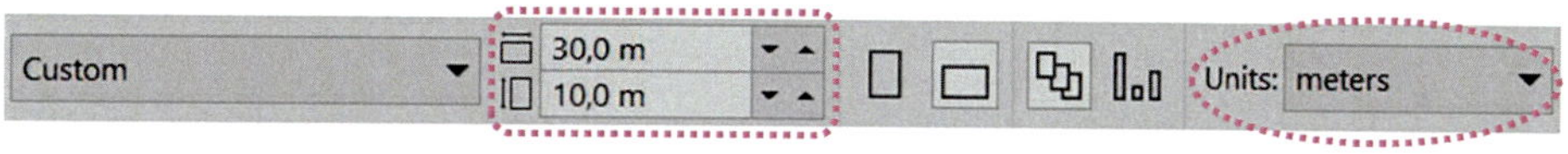

- Almost all (locomotive, windows, wagons ...) are simply drawn from rectangles, which were filled in color:

  - Locomotives with color gradient type linear "black-white-black" horizontally, thus rotated by 90 °, chimneys with the same color gradient vertically, see page 76).

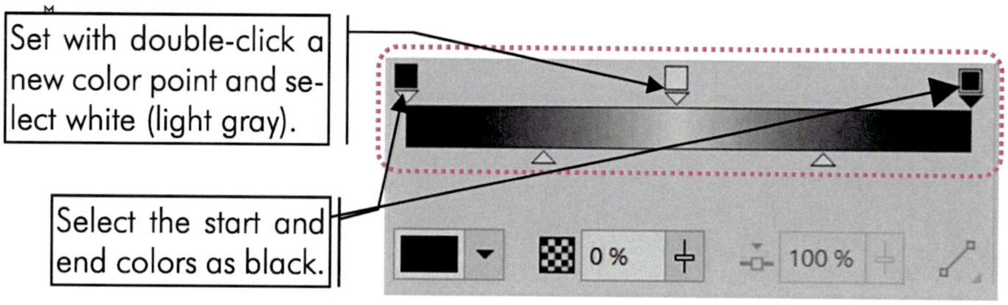

- Use the polygon tool for the tip, the stars and the first chimney, each adjusting the number of corners.
- We already created a wheel in a separate drawing; the exercise can be found on page 60. Copy the wheel in this drawing and duplicate it horizontally by pressing the [Shift] button.
- For the background, draw two large rectangles, fill the upper with blue color, and fill the lower green and place backwards (property bar).
- Draw the clouds with the freehand line. For this, switch off the grid and release the mouse only at the starting point so that the figure can be closed and filled.

Chapter 13

13. Special Fillings

➢ Using the exercise "Pyramid of Squares" highlight another rectangle and choose the pattern fills with the interactive fill tool.

Here you have these variants:

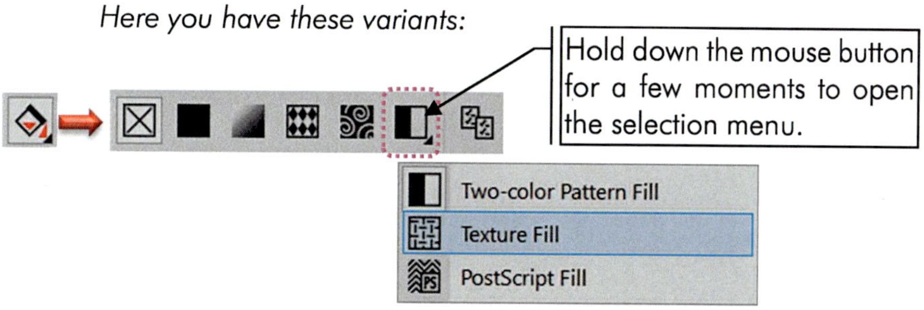

13.1 Two-Color Filling

- The fill pattern "Two-colors" is a painted pattern of only two colors in contrast to the colorful full-color fills.
  - ↳ The preference for two color is black and white, but you can choose other colors with the color buttons.
  - ↳ With this symbol you can switch to Texture- and Postscript-Fillings, too.

This two-color filling can be set up easily in the property bar:

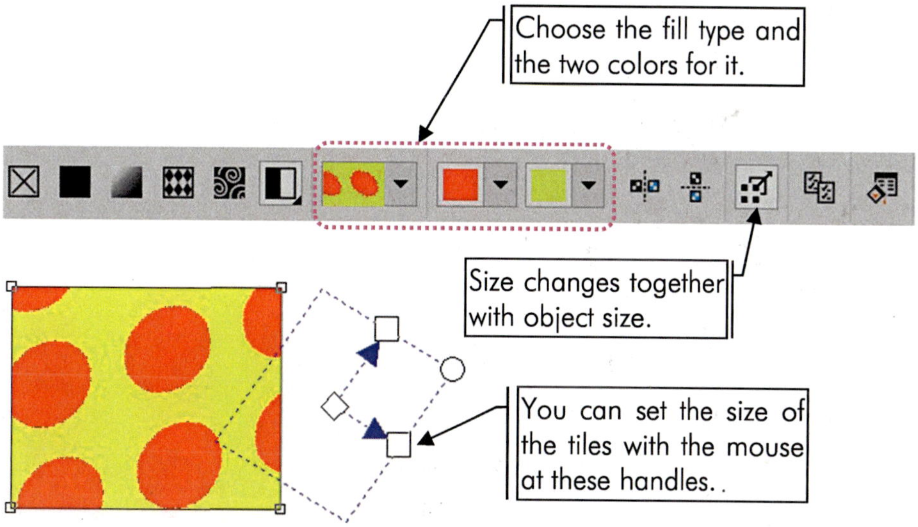

13.2 TEXTURE FILL – THE CORELDRAW FILLINGS

With Texture Fill you'll find the speciality of CorelDraw. Many of the Corel designed colored vector pattern fillings are very nice e.g. for a book title page.

- ➢ Switch from the Two-Color Fillings to the Texture Fillings.
- ➢ You can choose a filling type in the Property bar:

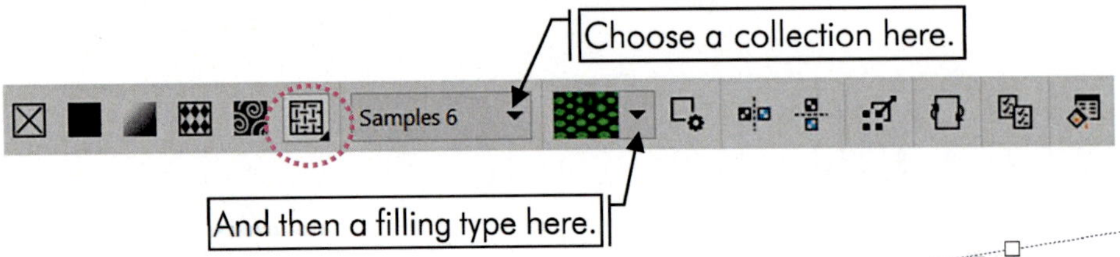

Looks different? Use Window-Workspace-Default

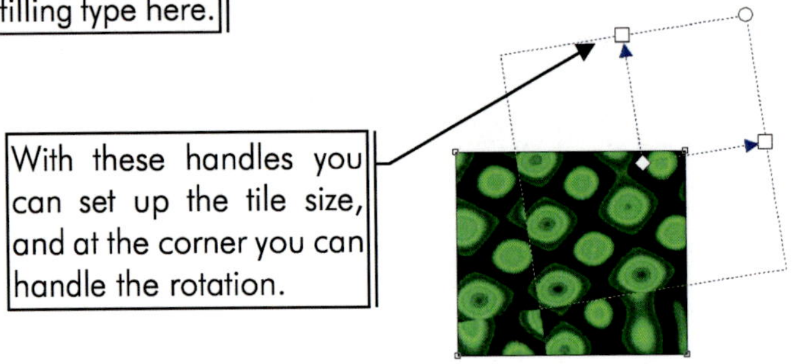

More setting options in the filling menu:

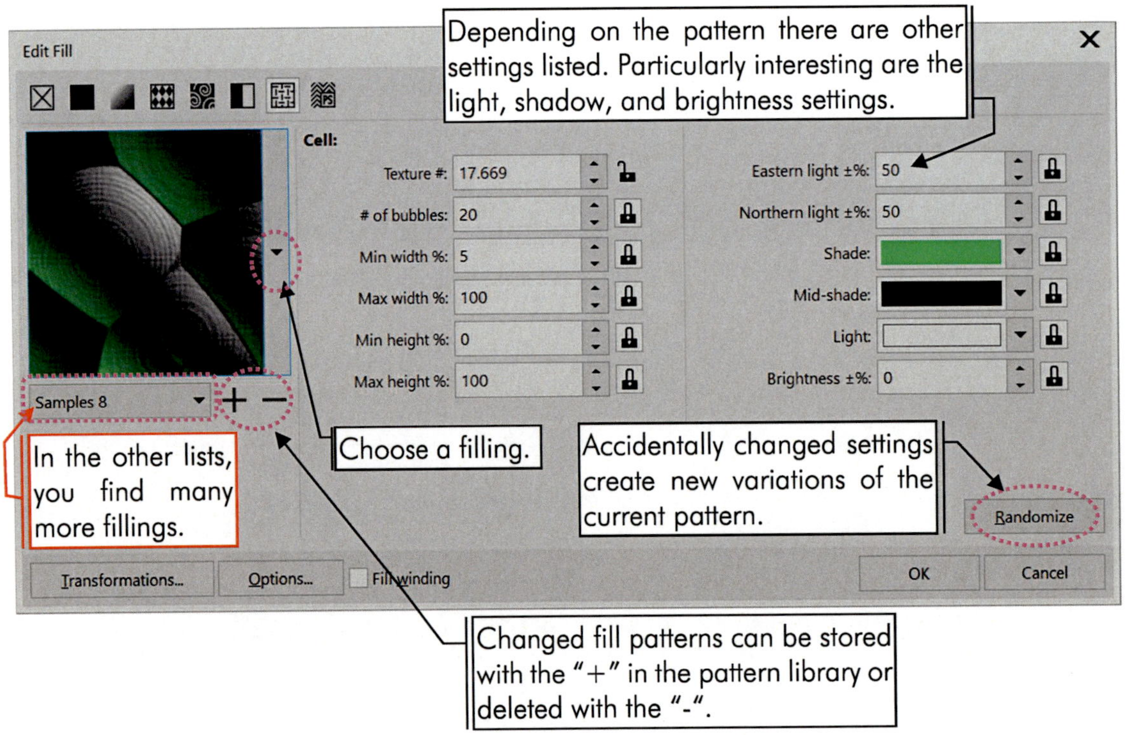

- ♦ Texture # and # of bubbles: click and try different variations of actual patterns, with more or fewer bubbles you have many possibilities for new filling patterns.
- ♦ Interesting also is the button "Randomize", to generate new patterns.

13.3 Postscript Patterns

Postscript is a standardized printer language developed in early 1980s from Adobe. The feature is that the print result is same between home office printer and print shop if both use postscript. Today most PDF formats use it for same result.

- With the two-pattern fill you can choose the texture and postscript patterns. You'll find some fillings consume less computing power.

➢ Look at the fill pattern; some are also colored.

13.4 Vector and Bitmap-Pattern Fillings

Here you'll find a collection of various fillings. Some are clippings of real photos and some are graphic work from designers, or both combined.

Here you have these variants:

- With Bitmap Pattern Fills, experts from real photos can be used. But it is also possible to find graphic work patterns here.
  - ↪ Bitmap, the file extension bmp, was used in early PC times by Windows for the Windows wallpaper images.
  - ↪ Thus, it is clear that we have to do it here with a pixel-filling so composed of points - with all the drawbacks, such as jagged edges.
- Vector Pattern Fills: graphic work fillings. The difference with texture fillings is that you'll find here fillings with forms e.g. circles, lines...

bmp

Assign a vector or bitmap filling:

Mark the object to fill and then the interactive fill tool-vector or bitmap fill:

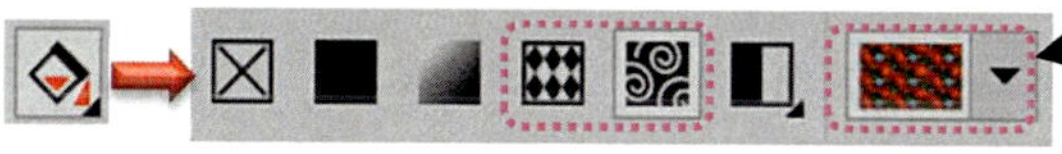

Choose a category on left side and then click a pattern on right side.

Please try them yourself. Here are some samples as overview:

Two colors	Texture	Vector	Bitmaps (Photos)
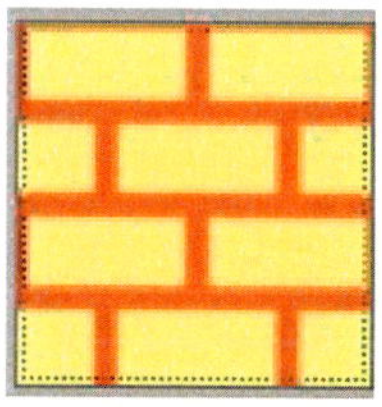			
	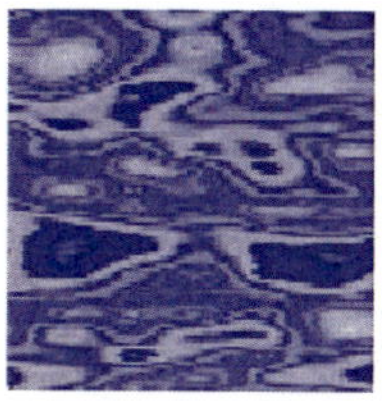		

13.5 THE TILE SIZE

The pattern image is usually smaller than the object used to populate it. Therefore, the filling is made up of multiple images (tiles).

Tile

- With the bitmap and vector filling you can specify size with the mouse at the handles. In the menu you can specify the size exactly:

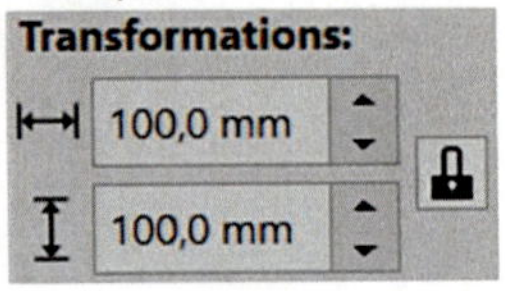

  - As long as the lock is pressed, both dimensions are changed at the same time.
  - In normal "small" DIN A4 or A5 drawings the tile size is usually reduced.

13.6 NEW BITMAP OR VECTOR PATTERN FILL

You can set each photo or an area from a photo or graphic as a new pattern. In the filling menu by bitmap and vector pattern fill you find these symbols:

You can mark an area from your desktop and set it as a new pattern fill.

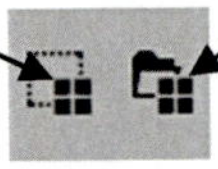

Load a photo from your storage media as a pattern fill.

- The left option also available by Tools/Create/Pattern Fill: then mark an area of your desktop and you can set it as a new pattern fill.

> Remark: the Home and Student Suite contains only 100 fillings, the Commercial Graphics Suite around 1.000. In Corel Connect you can download more fillings as actual installed, right mouse button on a filling and "copy to personal", then you can use this filling in CorelDraw.

13.7 EXERCISE: NEW PATTERN FILL

- Mark a rectangle or draw new one. For bitmaps, select the icon "New source from file". Now you can read any bitmap image.
  - Choose a picture from your storage media as filling for the marked rectangle.
  - If you can't find pictures, you can search in the Windows explorer with *.jpg for any photo saved in the standard jpg format. Choose the hard disk or "This PC" to find all storage media on your computer.

If you have a CorelDRAW DVD you can search the same way on the DVD for the sample photos.

Note: ....

....

....

Note the options below under "Import":

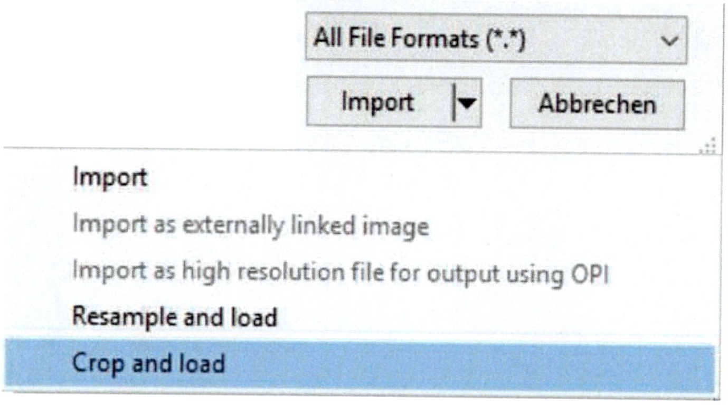

- Import: insert the selected photo in its original condition, most of the time the resolution is too high for a pattern filling.
- By "Resample and load" you can reduce the resolution, which is highly recommended for inserting bitmap fills, so the file is not too big.
- By "Crop and load" an image can be selected (with the mouse to resize the frame in the preview image and move), to use it only as a new filling.
- An alternative to the last two commands is that you can open the photo in Corel Photo-Paint and reduce the resolution and crop the picture.

  ↳ Important: don't overwrite the original photo; save it as a new file!!!

13.8 Copy a Filling

If you want to re-record the filling of an object to assign it to another object, that comes with the pipette. The application is done simply, bearing in mind the selection menu:

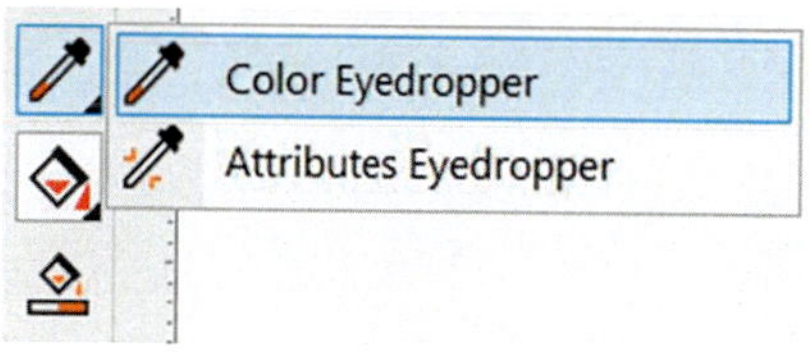

- With the Color Eyedropper you can pick up a color, but not a filling, and insert it into another object.
- A filling pattern can be picked up with the Attributes Eyedropper; hold the mouse button on the Color Eyedropper symbol and hold down as the selection menu opens.
- Alternatively you can use the command "Edit/Copy Properties from" e.g. to copy the filling from one object to another: mark the target first, then choose the above command and click on the object with the filling to copy.

Note: ....

....

....

....

....

Chapter 14

14. ClipArt and Shadow

14.1 Insert ClipArt or Photos

To insert clipart or photo's you have following options:

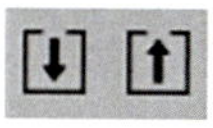

- Photos already stored on your storage media can be inserted with Import into your actual drawing, or
- With more overview per drag & drop from the Windows Explorer, or
- You can use Corel Connect: here you can insert a photo from your storage media or insert content from Corel cloud.

We use Corel Connect to explain the program content of the CorelDRAW Suite and to demonstrate the use of the content of Corel media stored in the cloud – if you have a Corel account you can use it.

- ➢ Open Connect, there you find Content Exchange e.g. photos, clipart and more.
  - ↬ If you move the mouse over a folder, a little arrow appears and you can open the subfolders by clicking on this arrow.
  - ↬ Click the right mouse button on a photo or clipart and you can import this into CorelDRAW or Photo-Paint.

Corel Connect with the folder Aviation:

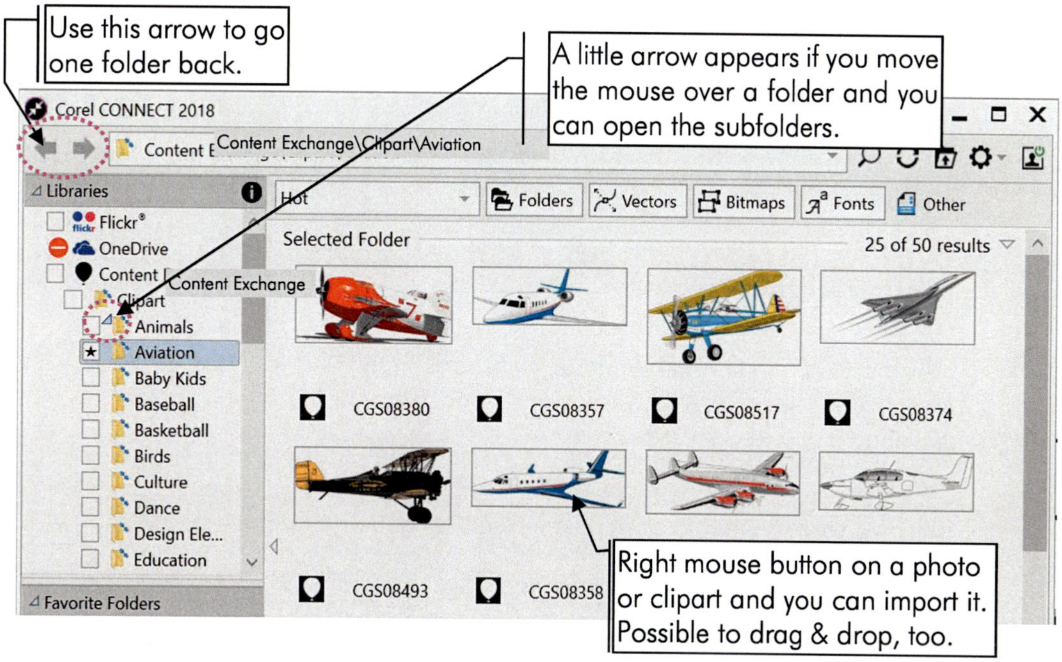

Notes on Corel Connect:

- On the top left you'll find Flickr, Fotolia, iStock (selection changes sometimes). These are online photo libraries. There you can search and download photos or post your own, some sites request a registration before using.
  - ↳ Usage in Connect: click on it and write at the top a search word; you will find many photos to each keyword.
  - ↳ Note the copyright of the owner – very important by publishing.
- At each window you can change the window's size at the edges and corners of each window and you can change the size of the areas at the border lines of the next area.

14.2 EXERCISE: BIRTHDAY INVITATION

A simple exercise. Paste a clipart, adjust its size, write text, add background, done. With the countless finished clipart choices, it is necessary to draw only in the professional field.

- ➢ New drawing with DIN A4 landscape. Pictures of festivals found in Connect in the folder "Special Occasions", add appropriate clipart in the drawing.

> Check also the other picture folder itself to get an overview of the clipart.

14.2.1 Background for Whole Page

➢ You can set a colored background easily by drawing a rectangle the same size as the page, filling it and placing it back. A prefabricated color fill was selected here (arrow in the preview image).

♦ If you draw the background first, you often accidentally get the background if you want to move an element.

  ✎ This can be prevented as follows: Right mouse button on the background rectangle, then Lock object. Unlock with same way with right mouse button on the object, then Unlock object.

♦ With the command Layout/Page Background you can specify a single color as the background or load a photo by "Bitmap". But a color gradient filling is not possible there.

  ✎ The "Print and Export Background" option is sometimes practical. If you disable this, you can use a background color to simulate a colored paper on the screen without printing this color.

14.2.2 Drop Shadow Tool

Now the text follows. As we apply our first effect by assigning a shadow to it, the effect of this effort can be better seen against the background.

➢ Write the text as two text blocks, then arrange and set them separately as shown.

➢ Assign a matching color or gradient to the text.

In the case of text, a deposited shadow is beautiful. Even a continuous shadow can be realized.

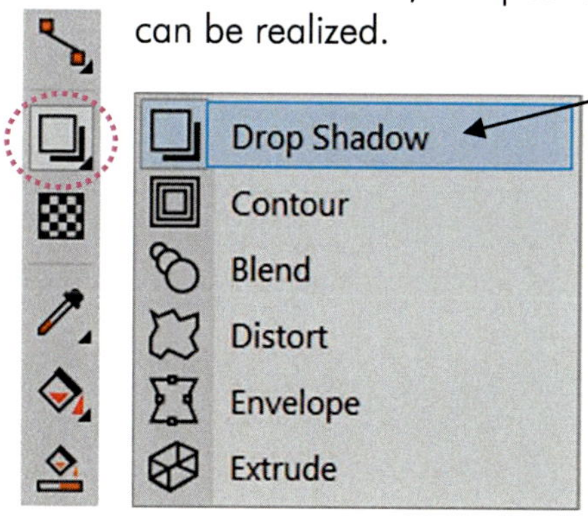

Open the selection menu for the effects and select the Drop Shadow.

➢ From the text beginning with the mouse button pressed, draw an arrow which shows the provisional shadow or, at the top of the property bar, a presetting, e.g. "Medium Glow".

Shadow with the mouse at a sample text:

Change the direction and extent of the shadow.

Change the transparency of the shadow with this slider.

The Property bar for the drop shadow:

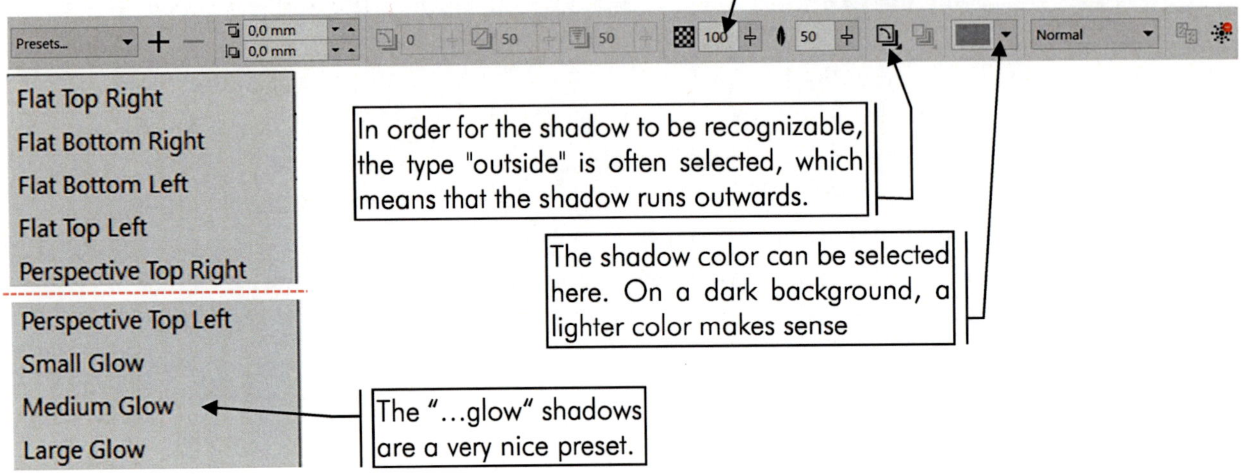

The opacity of the shadow is different depending on the color.

In order for the shadow to be recognizable, the type "outside" is often selected, which means that the shadow runs outwards.

The shadow color can be selected here. On a dark background, a lighter color makes sense

The "...glow" shadows are a very nice preset.

14.3 Insert ClipArt

A small advertisement as an exercise:

- New drawing with DIN A5.
- Import a matching ClipArt, e.g. from the ClipArt-folder Food in Connect, adjust the size and move to the right position.
  - ➩ At the bottom of the scroll list you can get more clipart with "More from selected Folder".

Set the Grid and use guidelines as edge markings. This helps to set the text to correct positions.

A shadow is nice for text most of the time. We have also added a shadow to the headline.

- Finally fill the text, arrange it and fill it in with color.
- As the background, draw a rectangle as large as the page and fill it. Here a radial color sequence was assigned.

Chapter

15

15. Interactive Menus

Interactive means that you can change settings directly with the mouse on the object instead of in a menu e.g. the direction of a color flow fill.

With the mouse, however, only the most important values can be set. All other settings can be found in the property bar or menu.

15.1 Interactive Fill Pattern

In the case of the interactive filling, all the previously described can be set in the property bar. Fillings can thus be easily assigned. Here are some options.

- Draw a new rectangle in a new drawing and select the Interactive Fill tool.
- Hold the mouse button while drawing and you set the start and end points and the direction of the color gradient filling.
- At last, you can define the start and end color.

Now, these symbols appear in the property bar:

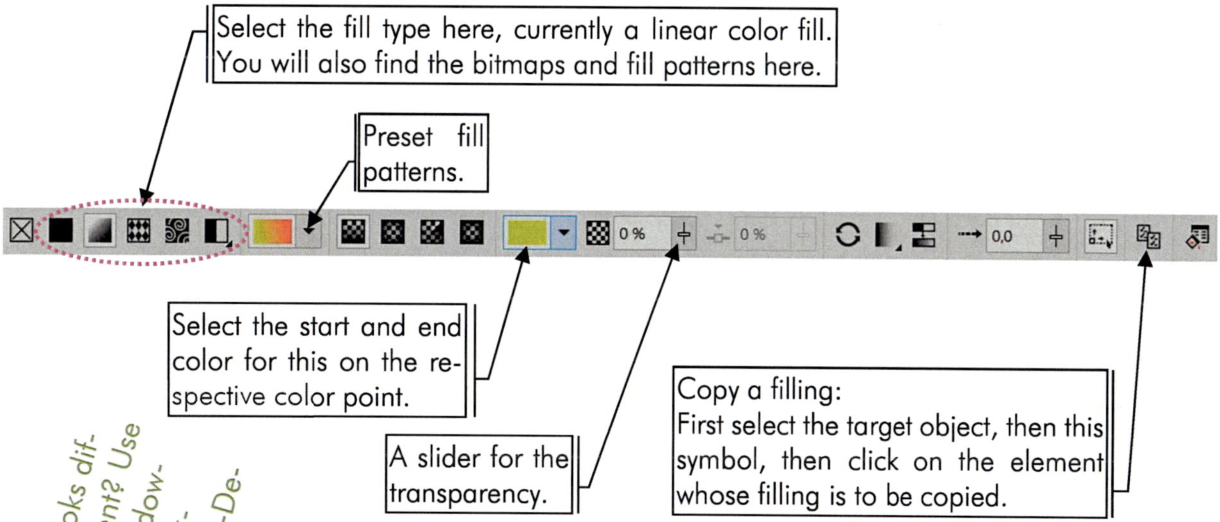

Looks different? Use Window-Workspace-Default

You can set the fill in the property bar or with the mouse on the object. Depending on the selected fill, other symbols are available that you already know from the previous chapters.

Adjust with the mouse:

You can also use the mouse to determine the starting and ending colors by clicking on a box of the color gradient arrow and clicking a color from the color palette.

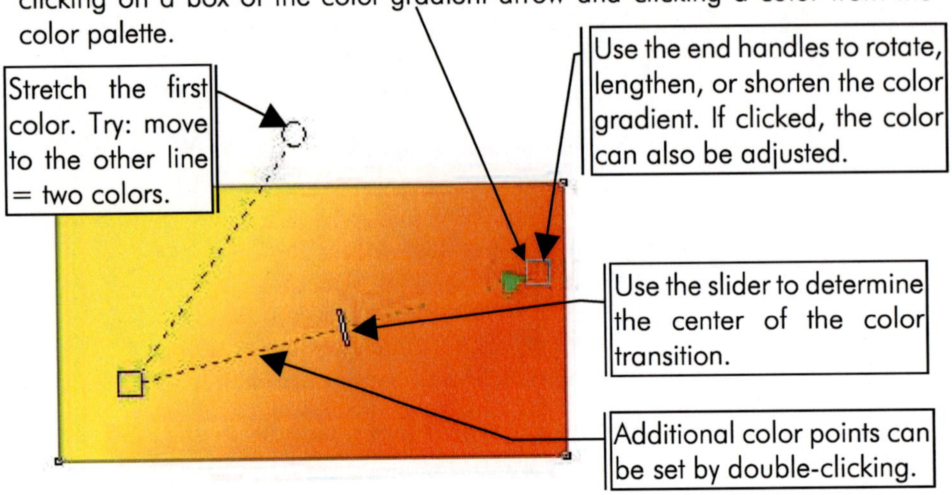

15.2 INTERACTIVE MESH FILL

In this fill method, a mesh grid is placed in the selected object. Then a color can be drawn into each area. A color carpet is created.

- ➢ Select or draw a new rectangle, then hold down the left mouse button on the interactive fill symbol until the selection menu appears and change it to the mesh fill.

A mesh appears:

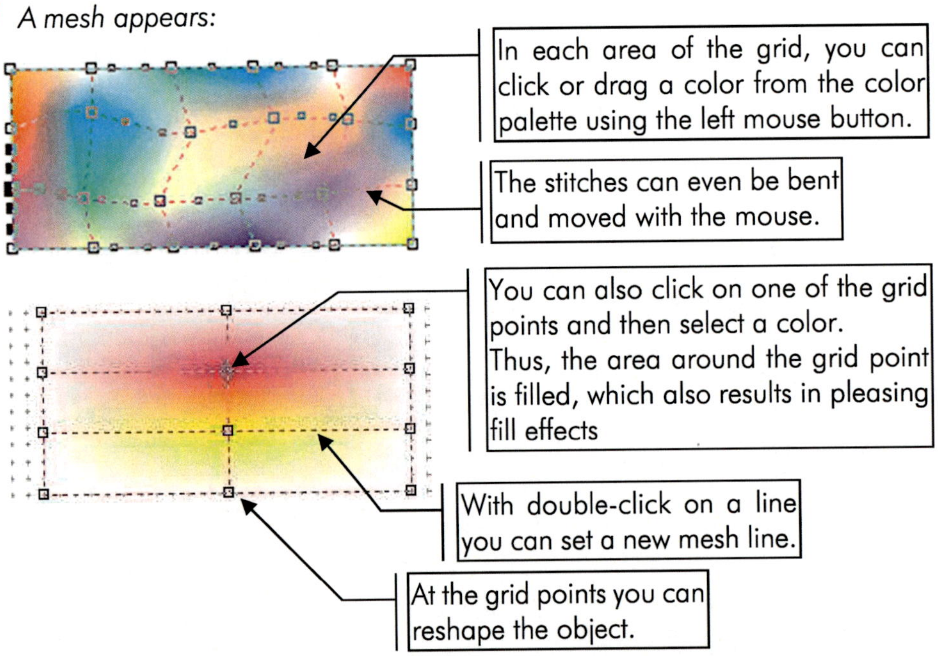

The following setting options appear in the Property Bar:

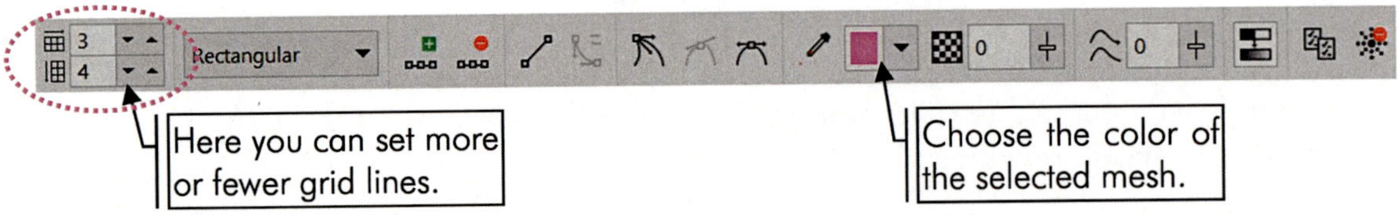

15.3 Interactive Transparency

In the Toolbox on left side you'll find the symbol for the transparency, so that the underlying objects glimmer through.

- Draw a new rectangle, fill with a color.
- Then draw an ellipse within this rectangle and assign it a fill color, too.
- Then choose the Transparency tool and either use the mouse to drag a transparency arrow within the ellipse or set the transparency in the Property bar.

In the case of transparency, fillings can also be selected as a mask:

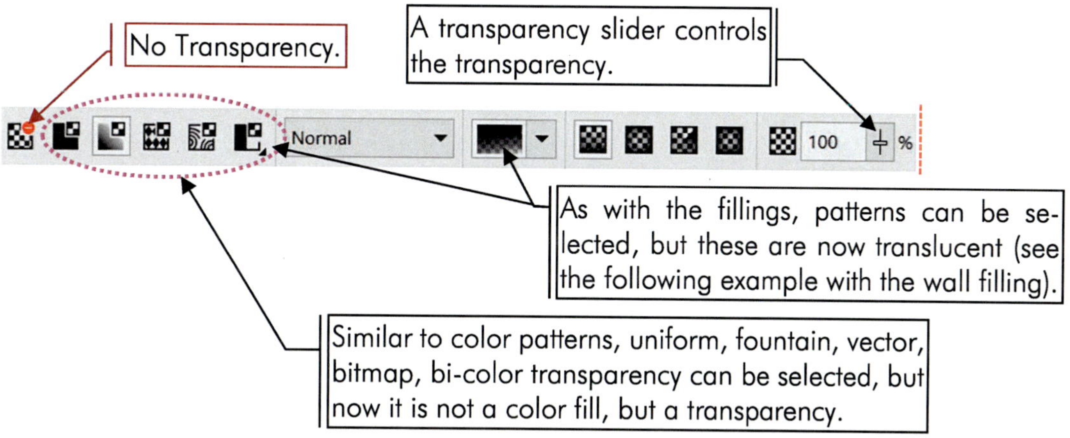

Right side of property bar:

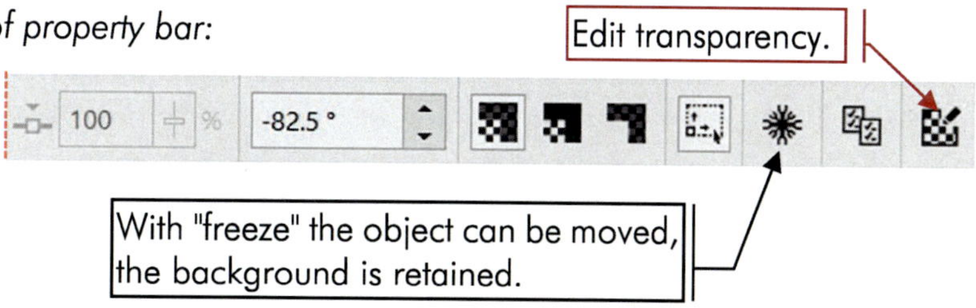

Transparency with the mouse:

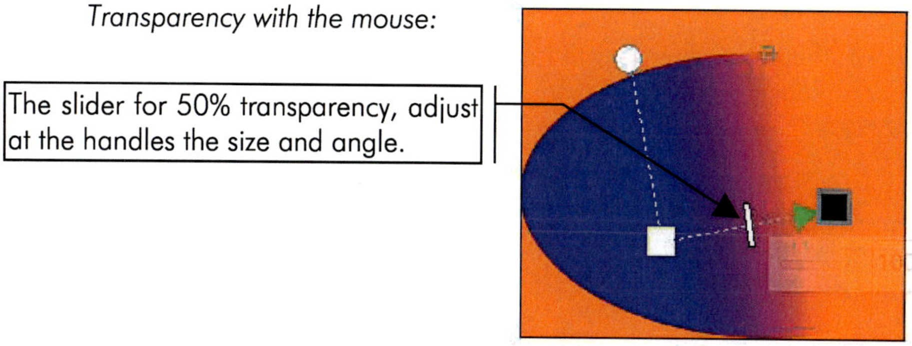

Transparency with the two-color pattern "Wall":

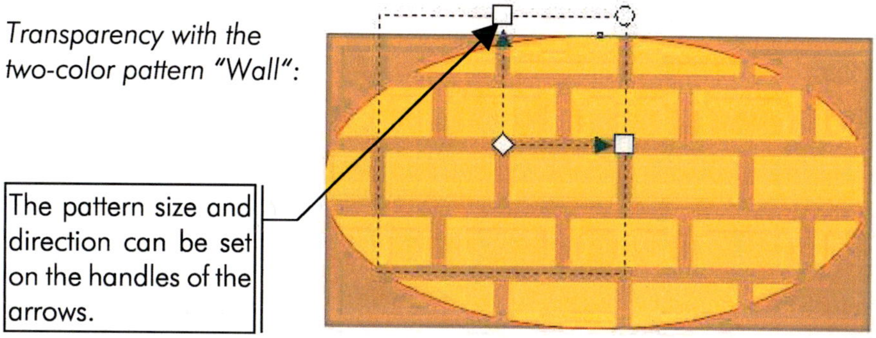

15.4 Inserting Photos

This interactive transparency is particularly excellent when the effects are used to make a photo more and more dynamic.

This is what we try to do with a new exercise. On page 89, you have already inserted clipart. Likewise, you can insert photos in Corel from the Corel Connect by right-clicking on it and then import into CorelDraw.

- ➢ New exercise: Drag two photos into the drawing with the mouse in the Connect and arrange them as the same size as the sheet of paper. Here we have used two photos of the folder "Landscape".
  - ↳ If Corel imports in separate instances of CorelDraw, you have to cut out the photo in one Corel and copy both photos into one CorelDraw.
- ➢ Then use the transparency tool to drag a temporary transparency arrow, then try the other transparency settings in the property bar.

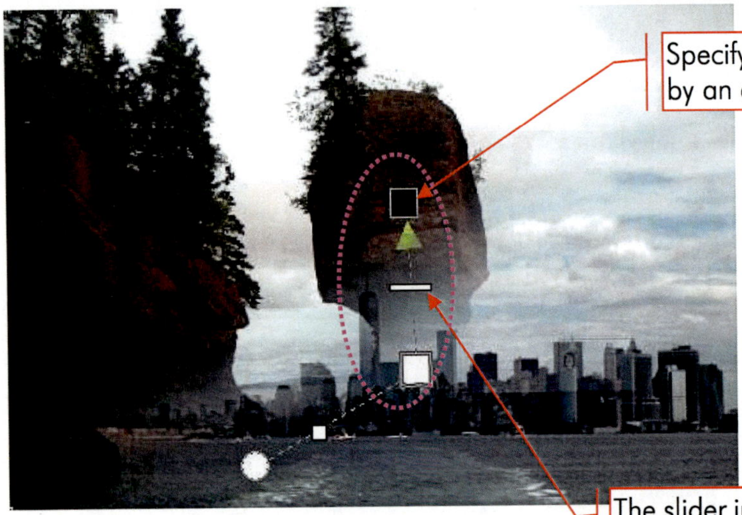

Specify the transparency by an arrow.

You can then move the transparency arrow as you like, or change its length at the ends, making the transition wider or sharper.

The slider in the centre applies to the centre of transparency (50% transmittance).

- ➢ In the feature bar, you can switch to other transparency forms, such as Regular or Radial or Pattern, instead of linear transparency.

Here, a two-color transparency was assigned to the above image and inverted, to see more of the city.

Copyright of images in this exercise belong to Corel.

Fourth Part

Shape

curve editing, text options and paragraph text

Something looks different? Use Window-Workspace-Default

Chapter 16

16. Curve Editing

- For the moon or the other figures in the following exercise, we need the Shape Tool for reshaping.
  - ↳ With this tool, we can change the endpoints of lines or the points at which a curve changes direction.

This is shown step by step in the following exercises. For the Christmas tree exercise on page 78, you have already applied the Form tool.

16.1 Exercise: Party

This exercise is ideal for practicing copying with the mouse, including grouping, multiple fillings, and especially curves.

This is how it will happen:

For the stars, the moon and the figures, the curve processing is necessary, an excellent function with which even difficult curves can be adapted bit by bit.

The background is a color gradient fill. To fill a page, a normal rectangle is drawn across the entire page. Then the rectangle obscures all other objects and has to be set backwards. So that we do not inadvertently move this while drawing, either fix it or draw it last.

Preparations:

- ➢ New file, DIN A5 horizontal, grid every 5 mm.
- ➢ A horizontal guide line for the floor so that all objects can be arranged at the same height.

The speaker:

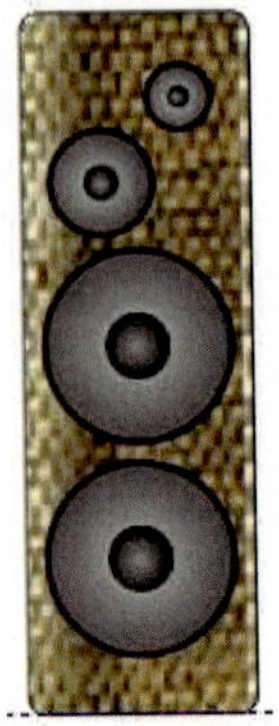

- ➢ Draw a rectangle as a speaker cabinet:
  - ★ Make it wide enough that in the middle is a grid row, so that the individual loudspeaker chassis can be drawn easily in the middle.
- ➢ Draw a chassis as a circle with a thick, different colored line:
  - ↳ Start in the middle of the chassis with the first point, hold [Ctrl] and [Shift] = Circle around the first point.
- ➢ Assign a radial color gradient fill, then copy the first circle in the middle and reduce it:

  - ↳ Hold the circle at a corner touch point, resize it while holding down [Shift] and click the right mouse button for copying.
  - ★ Switch off the line for this small inner circle.
- ➢ Group on chassis, then you can copy it easily and modify the size matching your imaginations.
- ➢ When a loudspeaker is ready, assign the fill to the enclosure and group it completely. Do not redo the second speaker - just copy it.

16.2 THE STARS – MOVE THE TURN POINTS

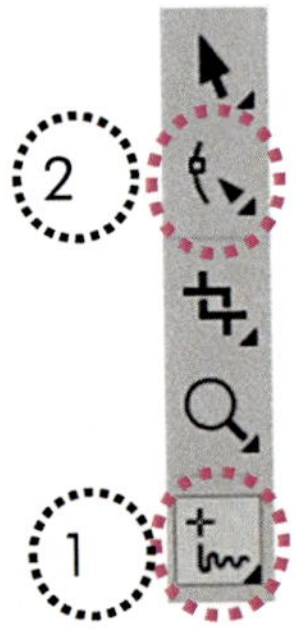

1. Draw a star: Deactivate grid, click start and end point once, otherwise double-click.
2. Now use the Shape Tool to move the corner points until the star looks halfway like a star (this can also be done with the Pick Tool).

- ➢ Fill the star, then copy the star several times, and rotate or resize each copy to vary their appearance.

This is a good exercise. But later you can use more easy stars from symbol fonts (see p. 66), or draw it with the Polygon Tool, or use the polyline (then only double-click first and last point, otherwise single click).

16.3 THE MOON - CIRCLE SEGMENTS

To draw the moon, we cut circular segments out of two circles and then connect them to one element to fill the moon.

- ➢ Draw one circle (with pressed [Ctrl]-button) and copy it slightly offset:

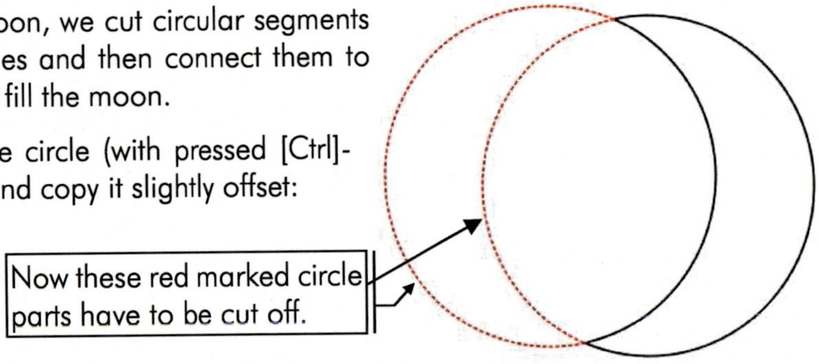

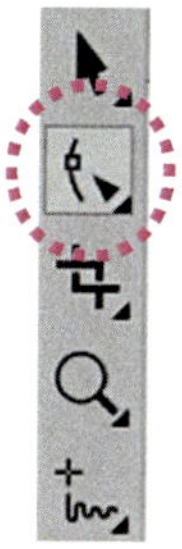

- When the Shape Tool is selected, click a circle. At the top of the circle, a small dot appears (not the eight handle points on the outside!).

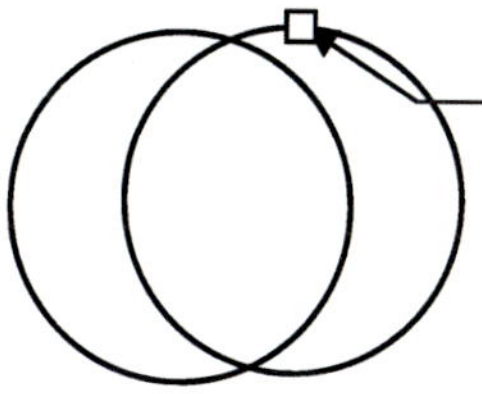

Open the circle at this small point a little and look at the line that remains.

[Ctrl]-Y

> Temporarily disable "Align to Grid" to allow the circular segments to meet.

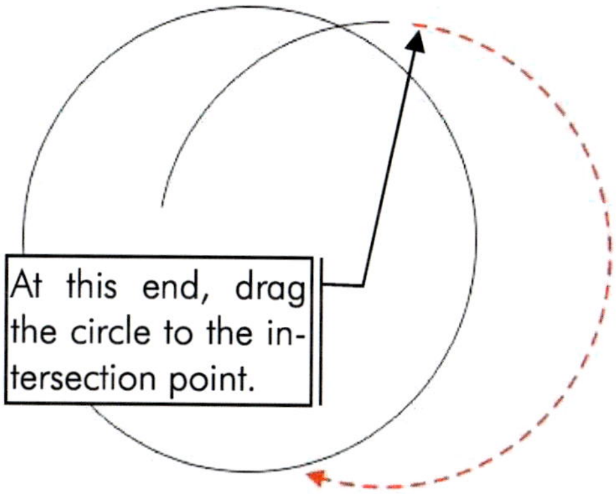

At this end, drag the circle to the intersection point.

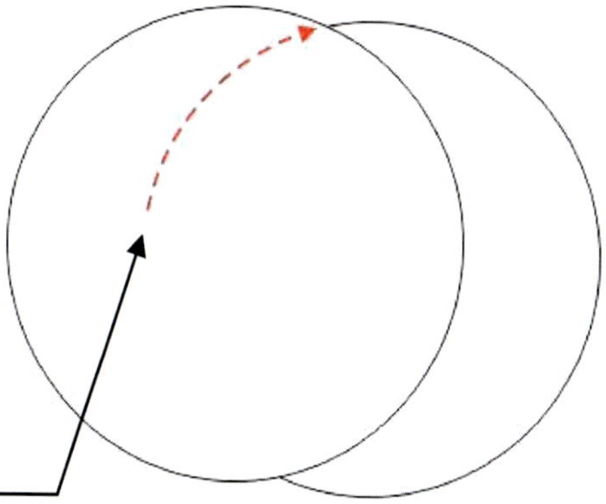

Almost done.
Now drag the other end to the intersection of the two circles.

Cake piece or bow:

Somewhere outside the circle let go, and Corel draws no lines to the center - a circular arc arises.

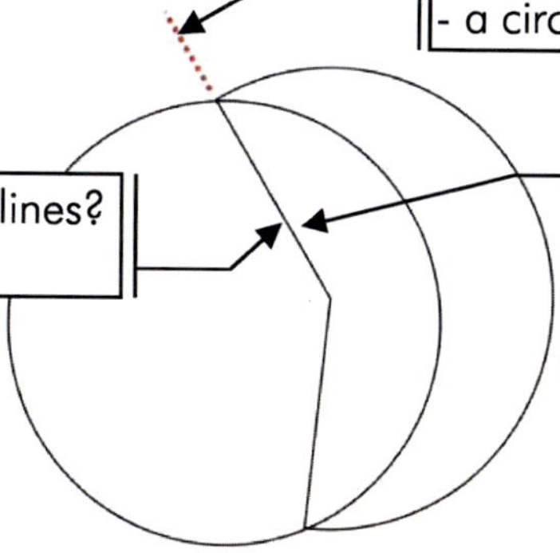

What are these lines? A cake piece?

Somewhere within the circle let the mouse go, and the lines to the center of the circle are there - a cake piece.

> No unnecessary thoughts needed to see which part is preserved. Open something, then see in which direction it goes.

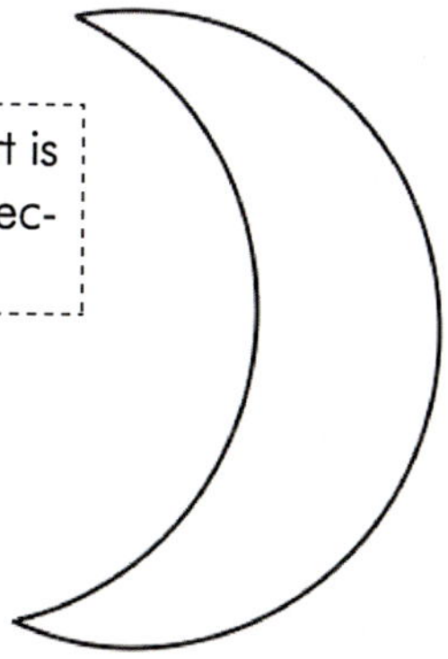

- Now transform the second circle to the arc and the moon is finished.

16.4 COMBINE TO FILL

Filling is usually not yet possible, because for Corel there are only two circular arcs, which have nothing to do with each other. So we must tell Corel that this is a connected figure, a moon:

- ➢ Mark both arcs and combine them.
  - ↳ This can be done with a symbol in the property bar, as soon as several objects are selected, in the menu with Objects/Combine or with Shortcut [Ctrl]-L.

[Ctrl]-L

For marking:

- ♦ If you press [Shift], you can select several objects by clicking on them.
  - ↳ As long as you press the [Shift] key, you can also delete a marking.
  - ↳ Note the message in the status bar at the bottom of the Corel window:
    "2 Objects Selected on Layer 1".

The difference between Group and Combine:

- ♦ Group summarizes objects to an element.
- ♦ Combine if you want to fill between two objects.

16.5 CLOSING OF THE FIGURE

In most situations, it is still not enough to fill the moon.

- ➢ Try it by clicking on a color of the color palette with the right mouse button.

Filling is not yet possible because the endpoints of the two arcs are not yet exactly met. Zoom in on the endpoints and you will see it in your drawing.

There we have the evil. But this can be corrected with the Shape Tool.

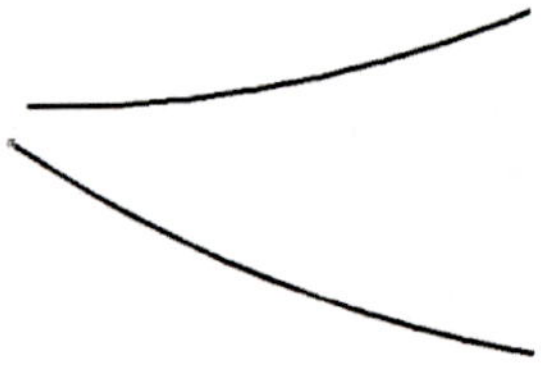

You can only use the Form tool if the arcs have previously been marked with the Pick Tool or are already combined.

Use the Shape Tool to draw a marker frame so large that both endpoints of the arcs are completely included.

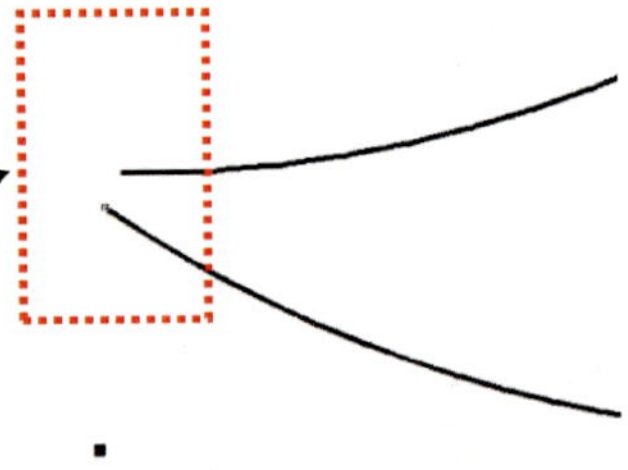

Now the necessary commands appear in the Property Bar:

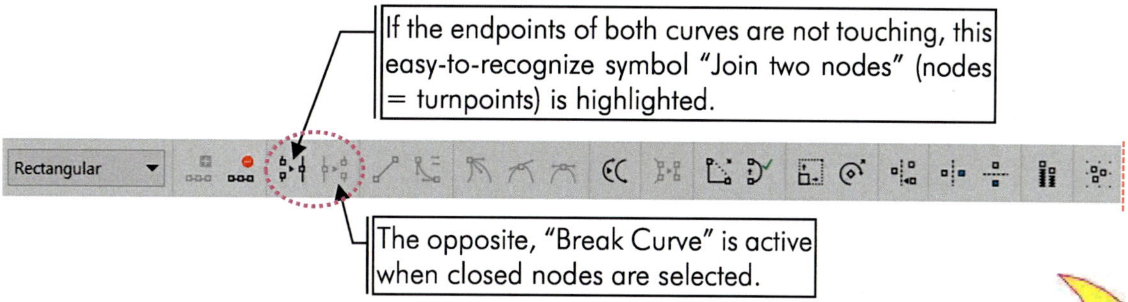

Is it time to fill the moon? If not, only these two sources of error can be considered:

- The arcs are not yet combined or inadvertently grouped instead.
- The endpoints are not closed. Check with a strong zoom, and if necessary repeat the procedure as described above.

16.6 Add Turnpoints for the Nose

The moon looks quite nice, but can be even more beautiful. We'll add a big nose.

> **Features of the Shape Tool:**
>
> All possible objects can be added or changed at any time. Even very difficult bodies can be drawn piece by piece.

- A turning point is already quite present in the middle. Click on this point and choose Cusp Node in the property bar, so that we get sharp corners and no round curves.

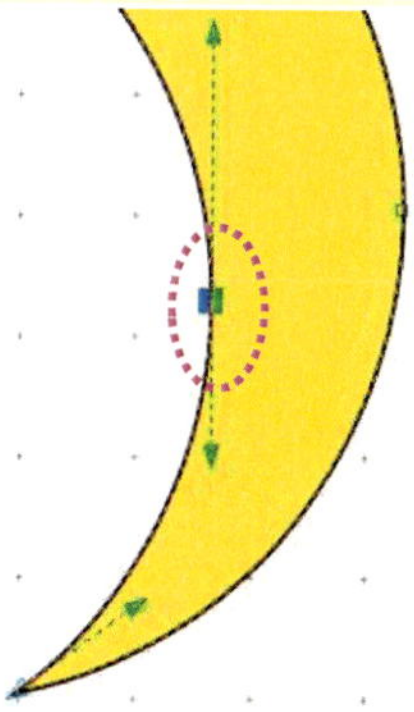

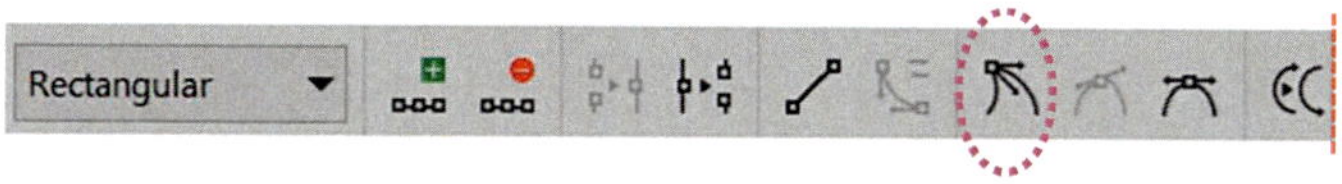

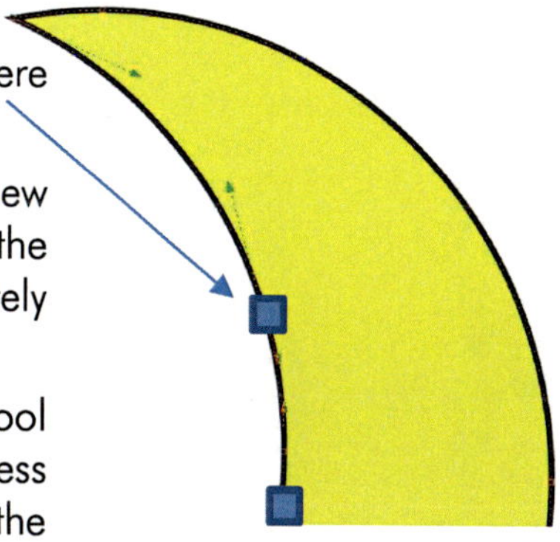

- We will add a point a little more here with the Shape Tool.
  - The fastest method is to add a new point by double-clicking on the curve line. This also immediately switch to a Cusp Node point.
  - Other method: use the Shape Tool to set a provisional point, then press the + in the property bar or on the keyboard for a new point. Only then is the turning point actually set.

- Now you can use the mouse to draw the curve between the two new turning points and pull it out.
  - ↳ Do not touch the two levers, since it is then double work, but pull out the curve in the middle between the two turning points.

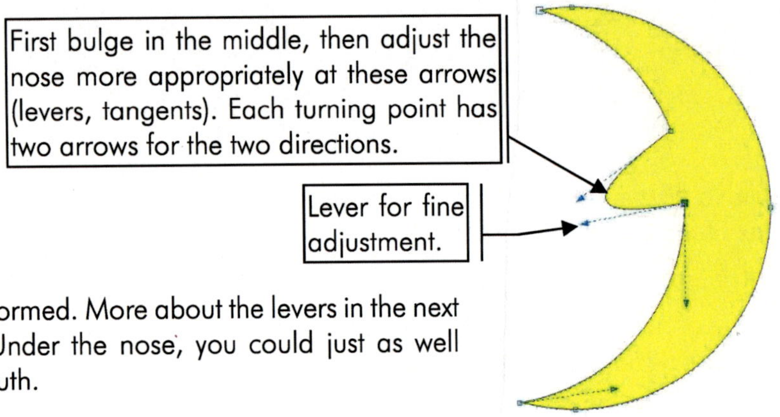

A nose is formed. More about the levers in the next chapter. Under the nose, you could just as well add a mouth.

16.7 The Figures – Adapt their Shape

Also, line figures can not be filled as long as there is not a closed line around.

Proceed as follows:

- Draw approximately the bodies.
  - ↳ With polylines or normal line and double-click.
- As with the stars, use the Shape Tool to make the figures close enough to correct.
- Try, if you can, to fill the figures.
  - ↳ If not, as by the moon, close the turning points with the Shape Tool until filling is possible.

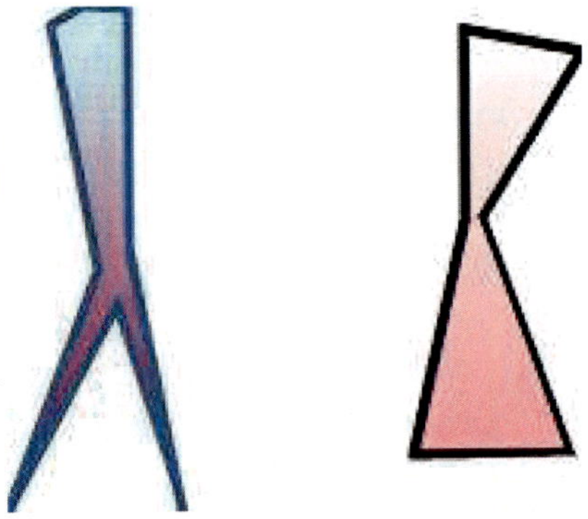

- Only when the bodies are already filled, then we will supplement the arms:

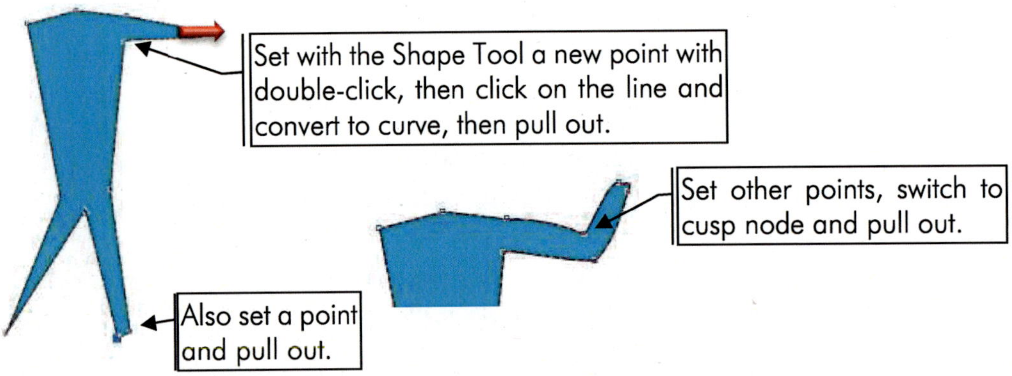

➢ Hands and heads (ellipses) at high zoom:

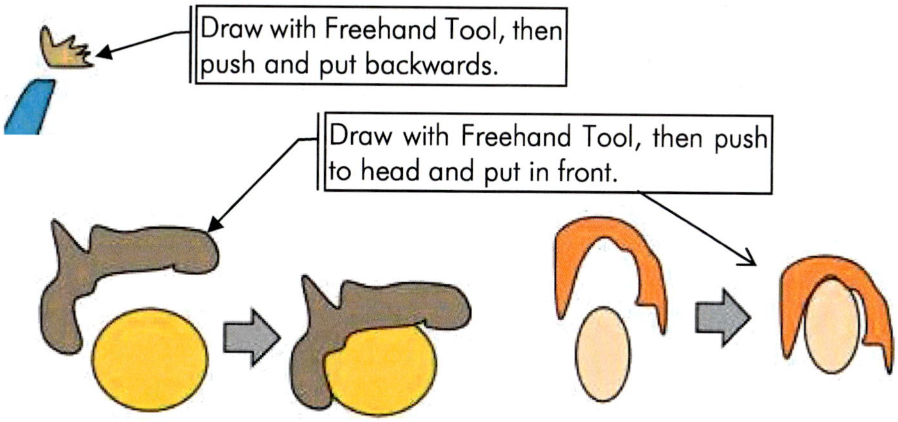

➢ We also draw the feet very simply with the Freehand Tool:

➢ With high zoom you can draw the eyes, mouth and nose with the tools you know (ellipses, freehand, curve lines) if you want.

   ➪ How eyes, noses and mouths can be drawn better follows in the next chapter step by step. Those who want can return to this drawing later to replace the eyes, mouth and nose with the later lessons.

➢ At the end, group each figure to make it an element, and the arrangement cannot be accidentally destroyed.

As an alternative, you could use characters from a symbolic font, or search for suitable clipart from the Corel clipart database or from the Internet

Also, symbols and clipart can be changed with the shape tool. Sometimes necessary to ungroup them before redrawing is possible.

Notes: ....

....

....

....

....

....

....

....

....

Chapter 17

17. The Snake – Curves Total

Compared to the snake, all the previous practice was only a small pre-exercise. But no fear. It will not be much more difficult; however, you will now realize how powerful the Shape Tool is.

- ➢ New drawing, size first 100 mm wide, 210 mm height.
  - ★ Set the Grid every 5 mm and activate align on grid and set guidelines as border lines by 10, 90 vertically and 10, 150 horizontally.

Looks different? Use Window-Workspace-Default

In addition to the curve processing for the snake, we will try the following functions for text:

- Insert special characters in text,
- Text with shadow,
- Align text to object.

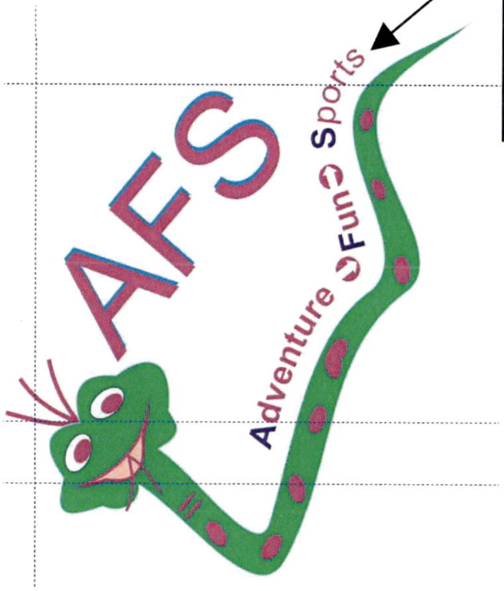

Adventure ▶ Fun ▶ Sports Ltd.
321 Pearl Street
New York, New York, 10038 USA
Phone +1-123-123-4566
Fax: +1-123-123-4566-50

17.1 FIRST PRELIMINARY EXERCISE

So that it is not too difficult, we begin with only one curve.

- Draw a straight line in the side edge, approx. 5 cm long.
- Click with the Shape Tool in the middle of the line.
- Because we have selected a line, the Convert to Curve button is active. Click it to make a curve out of the line:

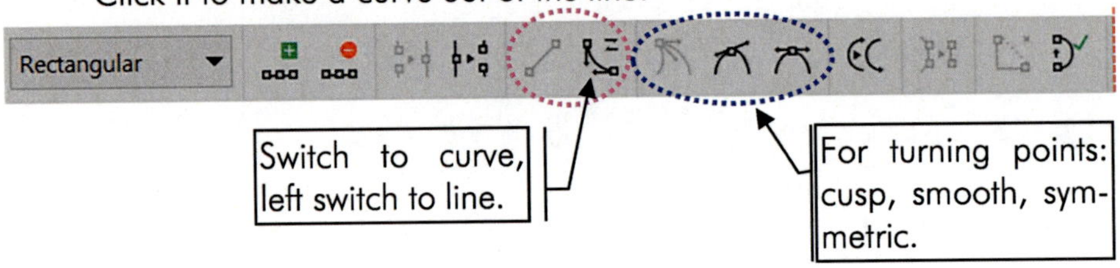

Do not hold the line by the levers, but rather in the middle and bend them to a curve.

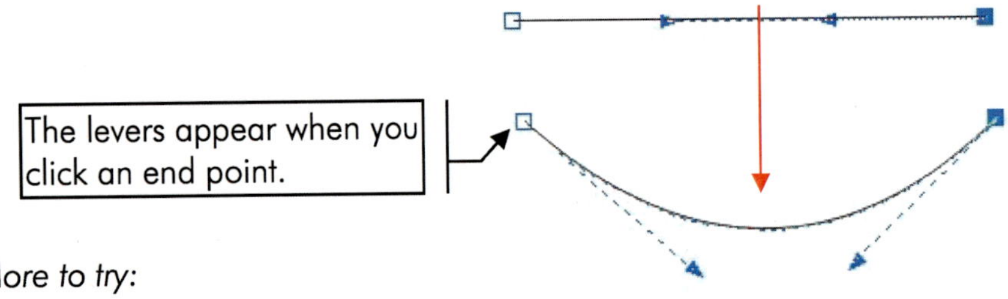

More to try:

- Turn one of the levers until the curve becomes an "S":
- Move an initial point of the curve.
- Turn one of the levers and observe the effect.

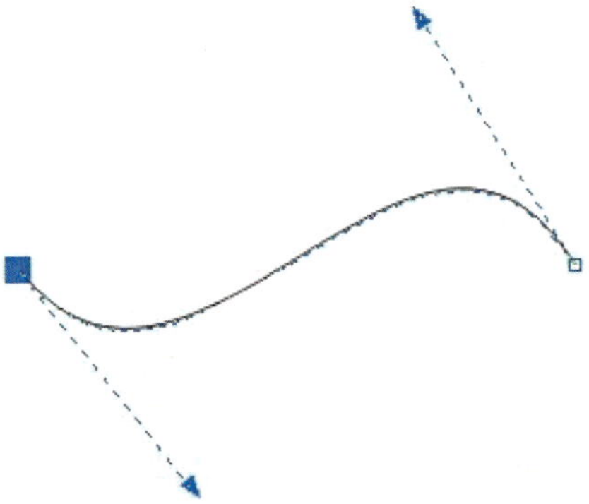

- Pull a lever all the way out - the curve bulges - and then very small - the curve is easy to bounce.

Levers

Levers are tangents! About the levers:

- Long levers complicate the handling in practice.
- In addition, you can see that two curves (S) can be made from one stretch.
- We therefore need only very few turning points.
- Too many turning points make the work much more difficult!

17.2 Second Preliminary Exercise

Now you know the levers a little bit. In the next exercise we go one step further.

Preparation:

- Delete the first curve that has just been drawn.
- Draw two lines, double-click at the intersection:

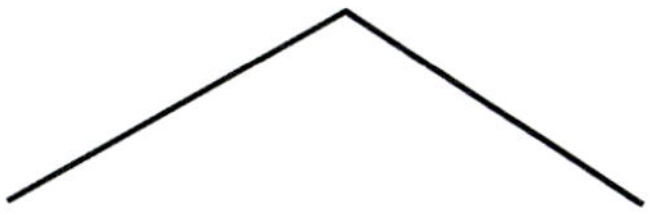

- Convert both lines to curves.
  - You can use the shape tool to draw a selection frame to select both lines at once and convert them to curves.

Curves without edges:

Now the point of intersection of the two curves is important, because there, finally, no edge should remain. This is achieved by aligning the levers to a line as shown in the following figure.

- Bend the curves as shown to make the levers appear. First touch the curves in the middle and bend them out:

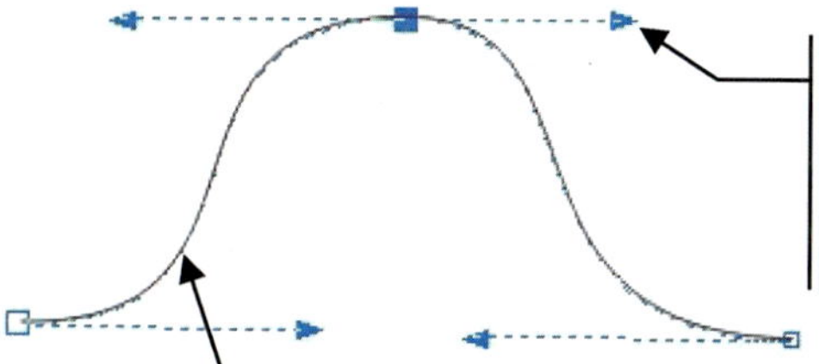

If you are straightening these levers straight, the curve has no kink, since the levers are tangents. This is automatically done with "Smooth Node".

Please note again:
A line produces two curves.
Do not draw too many lines on the snake! This results in too many nodes and that means chaos!

To exercise the levers, we have just smoothed a curve by hand. Corel does the same smoothing with the functions mentioned. If these are switched on, you cannot pull an acute angle like the nose.

Cusp nodes e.g. for the tip of a fish fin.

Smooth knots, ideal for the snake, since no "kink" is possible. The right is also symmetrical.

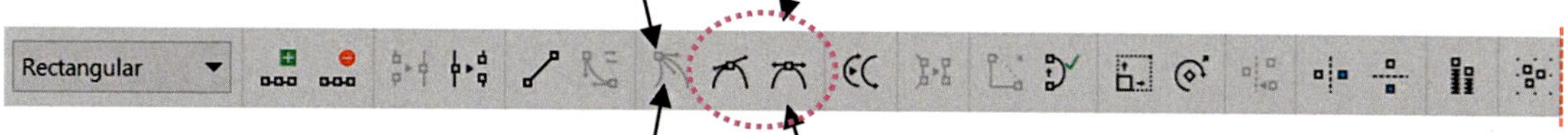

The current setting cannot be selected, so it is only displayed weakly.

Symmetrical as smoothed, but the two levers are automatically the same length. Try to extend a lever.

17.3 SERIOUS CASE: THE SNAKE

The snake is not a problem if you remember not to draw too many lines. Other points could be supplemented at any time by the + or with a double-click, but too many turning points lead to a chaos of levers.

You will see that the following figure with the red line easily turns into the green snake with round curves.

- ➢ Delete the previous curves.
- ➢ Draw the red lines by double-clicking on one piece.

The grid should be switched off for such freehand drawings.

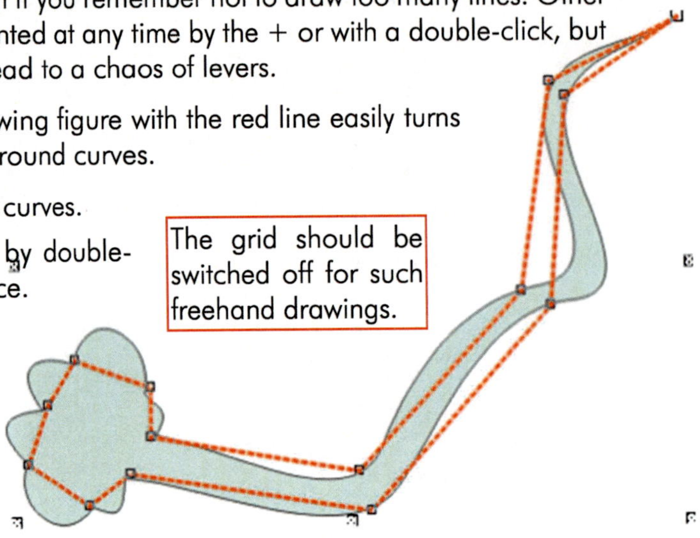

Either with lines = continue with double-click, stop with single click or with the Polyline = continue with single click and stop with double-click.

- ➢ If necessary, move the turning points appropriately.

Convert lines to curves:

- ➢ You can convert several lines at once to curves by marking them with a large selection frame with the Shape Tool, then switch to curves.

Select the turning points, and assign the desired type:

- ➢ On the head we need pointed points (cusp node), so mark the head with a selection frame and switch to cusp node (they are probably already pointed), and the same for the end point.
- ➢ Then mark the fuselage (without head and end) and select "smoothed" in the property bar. The turning points are automatically smoothed, and the desired round contours are created.

The function "smoothed" helps for nice round curves, only at the tip of the tail and at the head are some pointed points necessary.

- ➢ Modify the curves further until the snake shape fits.
  - ✎ The easiest way to do this is to touch the corners in the middle, not the levers.
- ➢ Save as "Snake" – we need this later again for making a flyer.

If it does not go as expected, there are probably still open points. Then close these points as described in Chapter 16.5.

What you might need:

- ♦ Add Points: with double-click (or "+").
- ♦ Delete Points: Mark the point and click "–" in the Property Bar or on the keyboard.
- ♦ Move Points: with the Shape Tool every time possible.

17.4 The Head and the Points

The head shape is designed just like the snake body:

- By strong zoom convert the lines to curves and buckle out.

The eyes consist of two ellipses:

The easiest way is to draw them first in the empty area next to the head, increasing this area as much as possible.

- Increase line thickness at the outer edge, both fill color. Adjust colors for both.
- Finish, then group to one eye, rotate and fit in the right place.
- Do not redo the second eye, but copy the first (with the right mouse button), then move and then rotate.

The hair is the easiest:

- Draw three lines, convert them to curves and bend them appropriately.
- Line thickness, color, and round end pieces in the line menu.
- Group the three hairs to an object.

The mouth:

- Draw two lines one at a time: Click, move mouse away and double-click, and return to the starting point,
- convert to curves and bend them appropriately.
- Increase the line thickness, select Fill and line color.
- If the filling does not work, close the points.

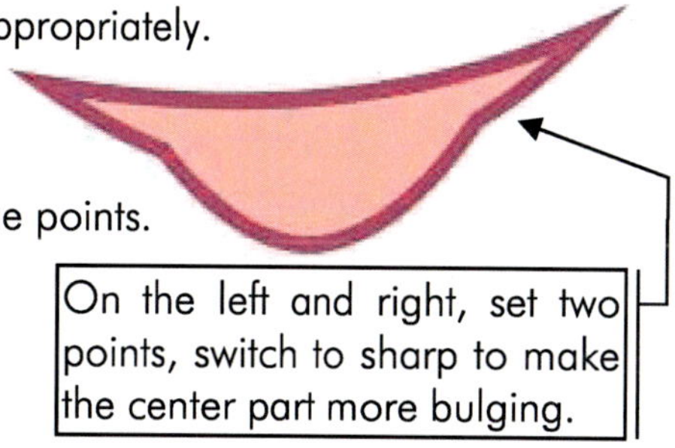

- Finally, supplement the tongue and group all elements.
- Now the mouth can be rotated and positioned correctly.

Do not draw on other objects, but

in a vacancy or in a separate drawing. Only when an object is ready, group it and move it to the correct position. Adjust the size and rotation.

We continue in the next chapter with text and pictures.

Chapter
18

18. Text Editing

Whether it is a poster, a cover page or a promotional brochure, text almost always occurs.

Corel offers two types of text editing:

- The Graphic text with the text tool (which you have done so far) for short texts that can be placed and rotated as desired.
- The Paragraph text to write longer texts as in a text program. Even styles can be assigned.

In the following exercise, we will supplement the text to the snake and will also fit the text to the snake as shown in the picture and in other various ways.

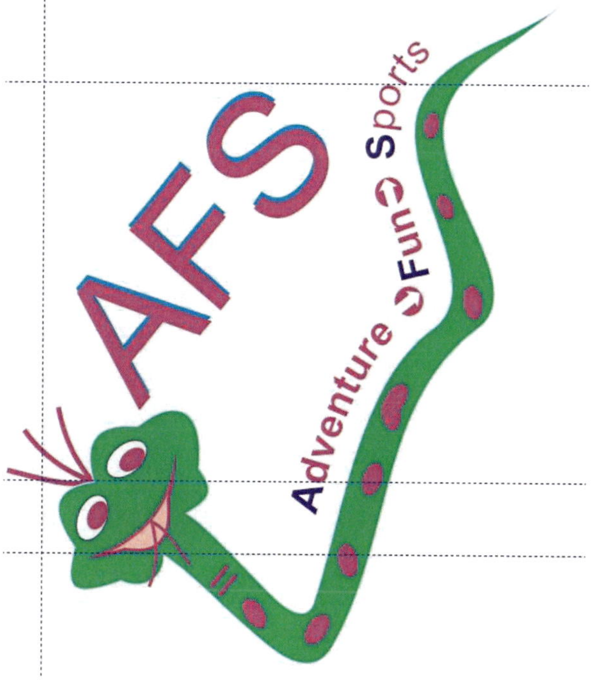

18.1 Producing Shadows

- ➢ Write with the Text Tool: AFS.
- ➢ Use the mouse or the property bar to enlarge it, but do not rotate.

A simple monochrome shadow is very nice and is used more often in professional work than special effects.

For this we will copy the text and move it slightly. Then the color is changed for text and shadow and the shadow is finished.

- ➢ For copying and accurate moving, the menu Object/Transformations/-Position is ideal.

With Object/Transformations/Position exact values can be specified:

[Alt]-F7

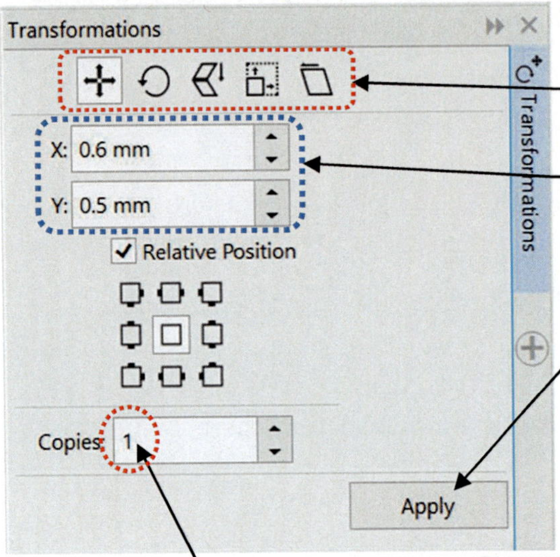

Position, Rotate, Scale and Mirror, Resize, Tilt.

Set horizontal and vertical offset, then specify 1 copy and "Apply". This gives you a slightly offset copy.

Press "Apply" to "0 copies" to move the copy step by step.
If you set the minus sign in front of the values, the elements can also be pushed back.

Move an offset copy (1) or move the object (0 copies) or multiple copies, which are moved by the specified posi-

- Move the new object to the back (Object/Order/Back one) and change the color.
- The shadow is finished, finally the two different colored texts can be grouped into one element.
- Write "Adventure Fun Sports" with two empty keys between the words because a special character will be placed there.

We want to turn AFS and Adventure ... at the same angle:

By means of the Property Bar, we can rotate different objects at the same angle.

- You can rotate first with the mouse approximately the way you want, and then change it to the next even value in the Property Bar, e.g. to 50 ° instead of 50.317.

Enter or correct the rotation angle.
A rotation can also be reset to 0°.

Even with the text selected, the rotation angle is displayed next to the text settings in the property bar.

- Without the Property Bar, the option remains over this handy menu Object/Transformations/Rotate.
  - ↳ Here, for example, set a rotation of 10 °, then press "Assign" several times until the angle of rotation fits.
  - ↳ The angle of rotation is thus known and can be assigned exactly the same to other objects.

18.2 Insert Special Characters

Now we insert symbol fonts between: Adventure Fun Sports

- ➢ Choose the Text Tool and set the cursor between two words (we have prepared with two space bars between the words).
- ➢ With Text/Insert Character or [Ctrl]-[F11] you can open the special character window
- ➢ there you can select a special font, e.g. Wingdings. You can drag a symbol on the text or insert with double-click.
  - ★ Move the cursor to the next position with the directional buttons and double-click on the symbol again.

Adventure ➲ Fun➲ Sports

18.3 Color Variety

In this text, the initial letters are to be displayed in a different color:

- ➢ Select Text Tool, click on text and mark the first letter of adventure, then use the mouse to assign a different color from the color palette.

Marking a letter, you have these possibilities:

- ♦ With the mouse, it requires fingertip feeling to mark exactly one letter.
- ♦ Holding down the [Shift] key and a directional key will make it easier.
  - ☞ And you can also unmark if you have marked too much as long as you hold down the [Shift] key with the directional key in other direction.

The color is only changed for the selected text.

18.4 Align Text to an Object

With this function "Fit Text to Path", text can be written to an object, e.g. at our snake. Let's try it:

- ➢ The grouping of the snake must be cancelled beforehand.
- ➢ Click on the text "Adventure ..." and select Text/Fit Text to Path.
- ➢ The mouse arrow changes to a bigger arrow, when you move the mouse near the snake, a preview is displayed.
  - ☞ Move the mouse near the queue until arranged as desired, then confirm with a mouse click.
  - ☞ The initial position and the distance from the route can be subsequently adjusted in the Property Bar.

You can change the arrangement at any time in the Property Bar if text and object are selected:

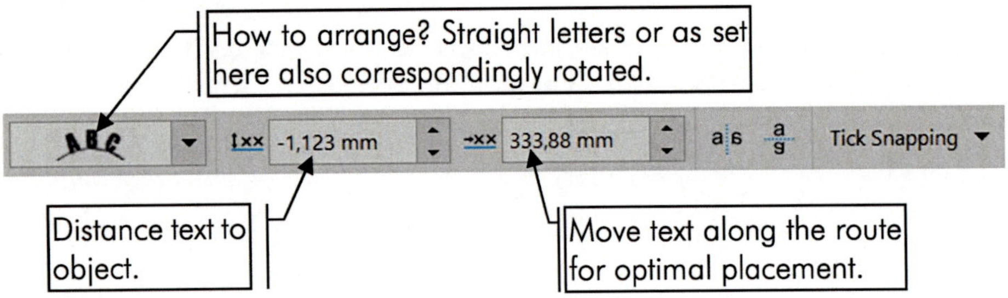

Tick Snapping:

- For example, if set at 5mm, the target position can still be freely selected with the mouse, but at a distance of 5mm, this locks a little, even afterwards during the movement.

If the text is placed on the wrong side, mirror it:
Text can also be arranged below.

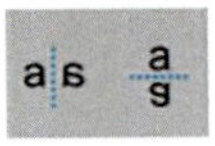

18.5 ADD THE ADDRESS

Fill in the address at the bottom of the picture.

- Ensure that View/Guidelines is activated.
- Write the Headline separate and fit left and right side to the Guidelines.
- Then make two blocks of Paragraph Text, align one to the left Guideline and text left aligned, the other to the right Guideline and the text inside right-aligned.
  - The feature with Paragraph Text is so you can align easy and exactly to left and right Guideline. With Graphic Text this is not easy to adjust exactly because Corel counts coordinates for the center point of it.

18.6 Other Adjustments for Text

The feature bar is very handy, but only the most important settings are available.

- The Property Bar for text you'll find in Chapter 10.1.1.
- The complete menu with all settings for text can be found on these paths:
  - right mouse button on the text, then Object Properties
  - or open with Window/Toolbar/Text the toolbar for text
  - or Text/Text Properties: in this menu you will also find the position or fractional numbers,

  - the shortcut **[Ctrl]-T** opens this menu, too,
  - or use the symbol in the Property Bar to see left border.

The Docker Text/Text Properties:

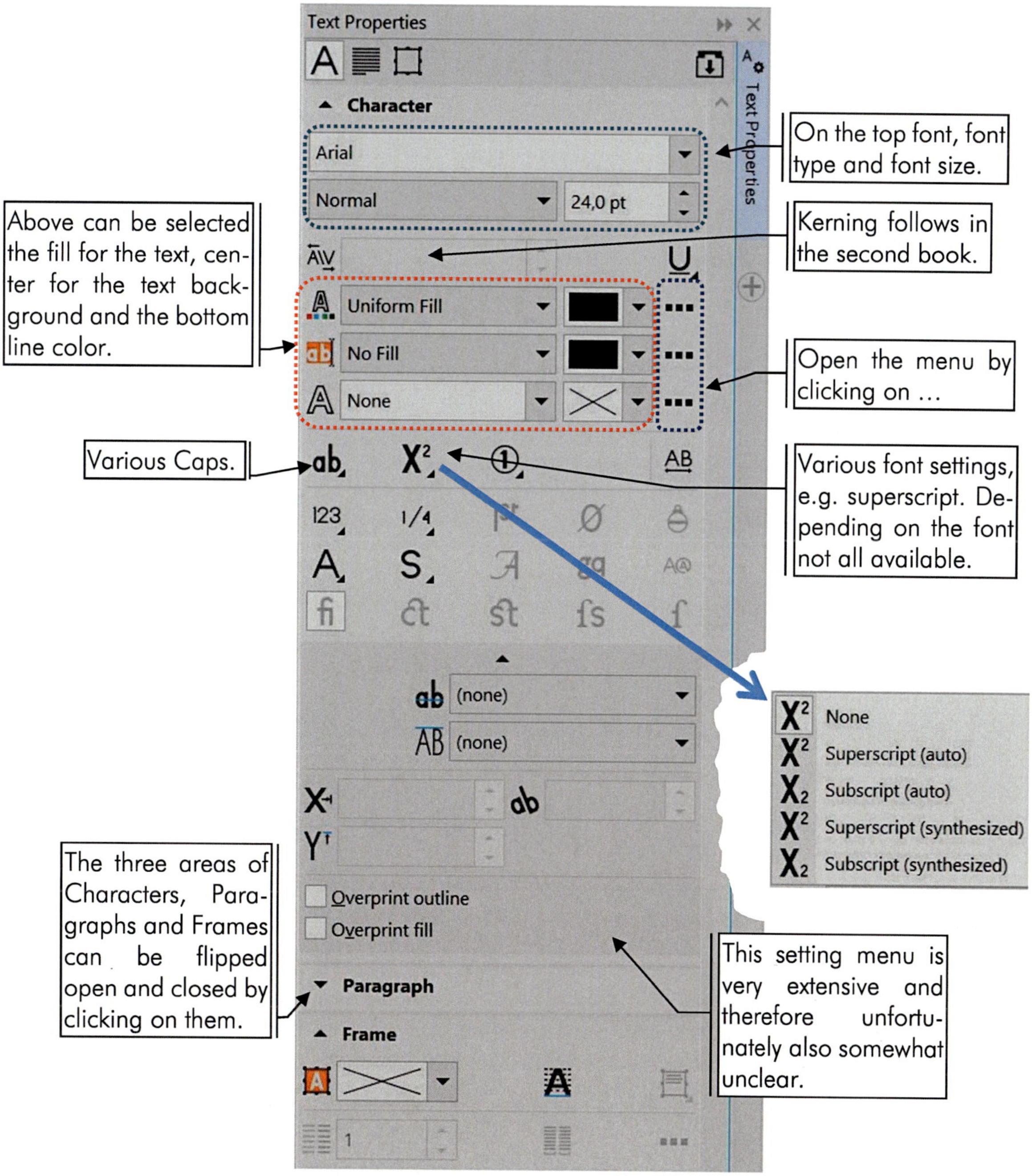

Now we still need paragraph formatting, this mostly applies to Paragraph text:

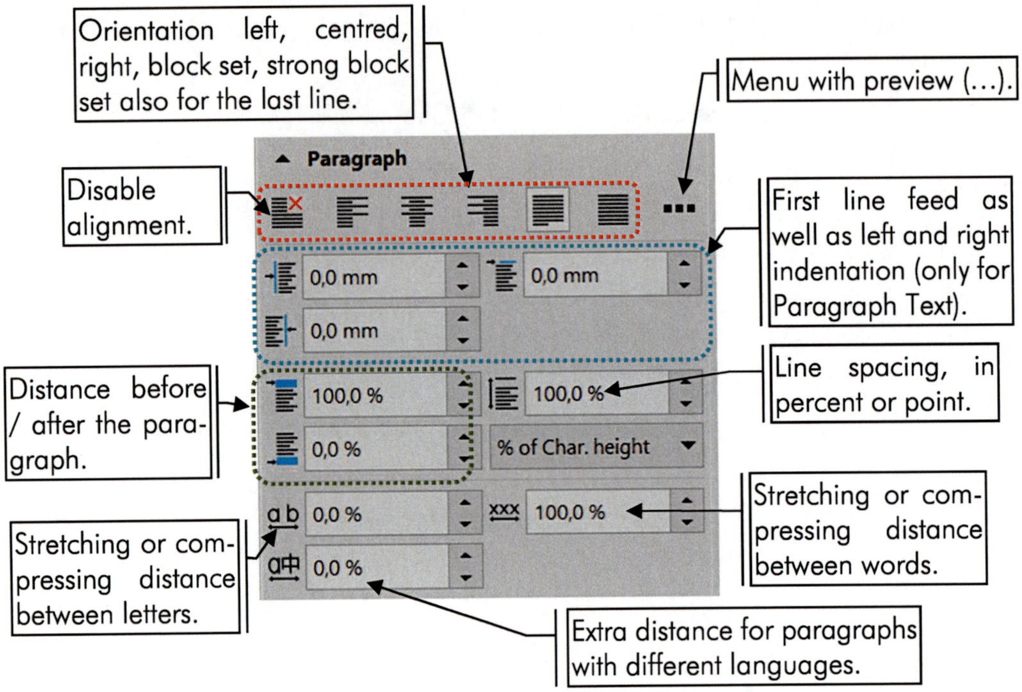

More about the text settings:

- The setting in percentage of the character size has the advantage that the setting is adapted automatically if you change the font size.
- Depending on the font selected, not all options are possible, e.g. some fonts cannot be set bold or italic.
- Text/Text Properties, [Ctrl]-[Shift]-T or in the Property Bar ab| opens a small text screen (text editor) in which you can correct, write and format the text - helpful if the text is distorted with effects.

Ctrl-Shift-T

18.7 OTHER TEXT HELPS

- Corel provides all the tools of a good word processing program that you will find in Text/Writing Tools:
  - a Spell Checker,
  - a Grammar Checker and
  - Thesaurus, a dictionary for synonyms. Here you can search for similar terms to a word.
  - the QuickCorrect, which opens a window in which this automatic correction can be adjusted,
  - the language can also be chosen here so that the spelling check also works for foreign-language texts,
  - by Tools/Options/Text, some writing aids can be adjusted, e.g. whether manual corrections should be automatically added to the QuickCorrect.

About QuickCorrect:

The QuickCorrect is similar the AutoCorrekt in MS Word.

- With "Capitalize first letter of sentences" the first letter of a sentence is also capitalized after each abbreviation, since CorelDRAW starts a new sentence after each point. This option is disabled for Corel X7 by default. If the capitalization is corrected once after an abbreviation, Corel accepts this.
- With "Change straight quotes to typographic quotes" Corel changes to "abc" instead of "abc".
- "Replace text while typing" automatically replaces the standard errors in the list below with the entered texts.
  - ✎ Other abbreviations, e.g. for a company name, can be supplemented. In the case of "Replace:", enter an abbreviation or an incorrect spelling, enter the detailed or correct spelling in "With:" and save it with "Add".
  - ✎ If you often have unwanted replacements, you should disable this feature. If you want to use this function, it is worthwhile to maintain the replacement list.

Note: ....

Chapter 19

19. The Paragraph Text

Paragraph text is the second type of text editing in CorelDRAW. While graphic text behaves as a drawing element, paragraph text is arranged in a text frame.

Paragraph text is, so to speak, a small text program, which we can open in a Corel graphic. This text is set within a frame for the delineation.

paragraph text for big amounts of text.

You start the Paragraph Text as follows:

- Press as usual the text symbol. Then:
  - ➯ Click in the drawing to write Graphic Text or
  - ➯ Draw a Paragraph Text frame like a rectangle with the mouse button pressed.

- Caution, do not draw empty Paragraph Text frames!
  - ➯ Draw a Paragraph frame only if this is the intention.
  - ➯ Otherwise, immediately switch back from the Text Tool to the Pick Tool arrow, otherwise you would use the text tool instead of the Pick Tool and create an empty text frame.

Empty quantity text frames are indicated by dashed lines. Delete any accidentally drawn frames: Click on it with Pick Tool – [Del].

Empty Paragraph Text frames:

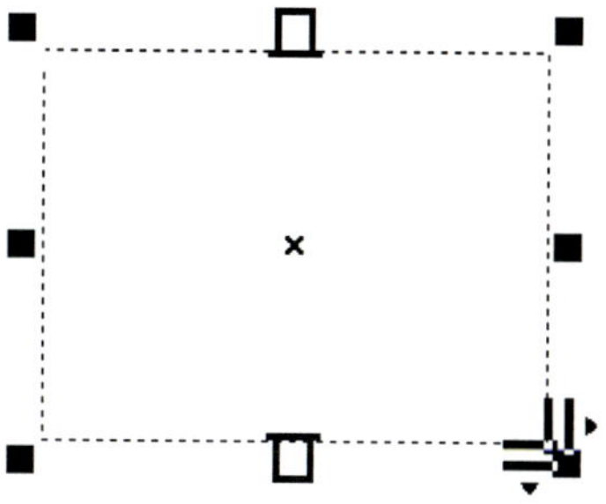

Paragraph Text frames with text:

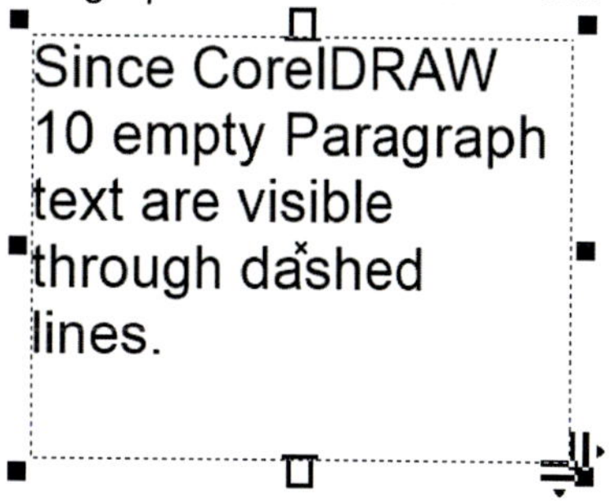

19.1 Converting Text

This is displayed in the Text Menu, in the scrolling menu with the right mouse button or with the keyboard truncation [Ctrl]-F8.

[Ctrl]-F8

Conditions:

- Mark the text with the Pick Tool, not with the Text Tool.
- With Paragraph text, the text frame does not have to be so big that the text is completely visible.

19.2 EXERCISE: BUSINESS CARD

To get a better understanding of the Paragraph Text, we will create a small business card. This is how it will go:

New drawing, size 80X60 mm, adjust the grid to 1 mm distance – for a small drawing we need a fine grid distance.

Because we are printing on colored paper, we choose a paper color:

- ➢ Layout/Page Background, then choose with "Solid:" the color palette Pantone CMYK Coated by Process.

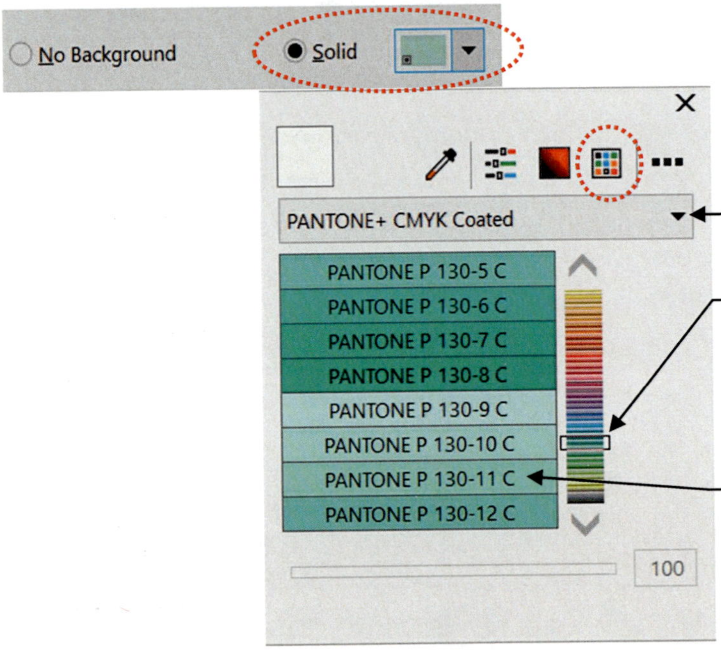

Chose here a Pantone-Palette.

Make a pre-selection in the color bar, then click a color on the left.

For example, if you use the color number, e.g. in the side margin and forward it to the printing office, the color exactly matches.

- ➢ Switch off "Print and Export Background", so that the set paper color is not printed – the print shop will use paper in this color.
  - ➯ It is a good practice to better assess ink composition on the screen when printing on colored paper.

The two lines above and below are simple rectangles with a color gradient fill:

- ➢ Place the Guidelines 4 mm apart from the side edge.
- ➢ Draw a rectangle, turn the outline off (with the right mouse button at the top of the color palette with the X) and
- ➢ fill with a gradient color filling similar to the one shown.

Now we will copy and flip the rectangle once, which gives the copy a precisely swapped color fill (Object/Transformations/Scale and Mirror).

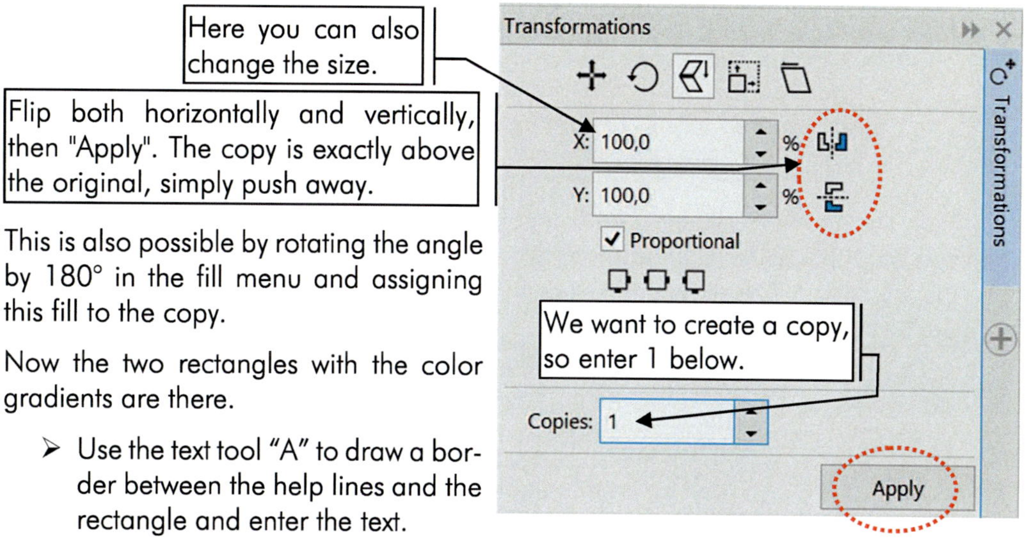

This is also possible by rotating the angle by 180° in the fill menu and assigning this fill to the copy.

Now the two rectangles with the color gradients are there.

➢ Use the text tool "A" to draw a border between the help lines and the rectangle and enter the text.

  ↳ Since this frame is docked to the left and right of the help lines, the centering of the text is easier than with the graphic text.

19.3 HANDLING WITH THE PARAGRAPH TEXT FRAMES

- Too much or too big of text or a too small text frame will cause the text to be displayed only partially or not.
  - ↳ Always pull the frame down and right much larger than necessary until the text is set correctly. Only if the text is finished, then reduce the size of the text frame.
  - ↳ An alternative is the command "Text/Paragraph Text Frame/Fit Text to Frame", also accessible by right-clicking on the frame, so the font size is automatically adjusted so that the text fills the frame.

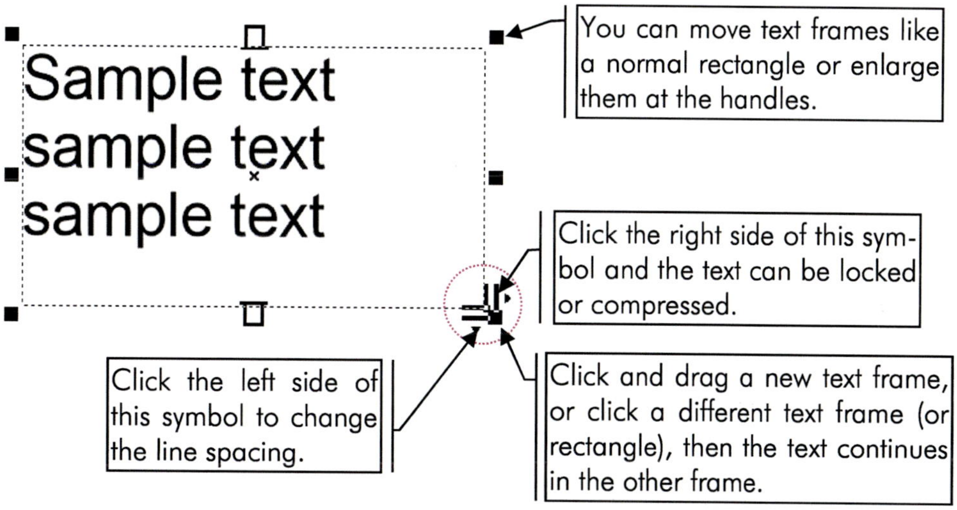

➢ Format the business card as shown. Always select the appropriate text.

19.4 Print from CorelDraw

As in any program, you can print on these paths:
File/Print / with the Symbol / [Ctrl]-P.

- On the tab "General", the printer can be selected and the desired print quality can be set by "Preferences…".
  - ↳ With "Page:" you can choose Landscape or Portrait.

With the "Home & Student" Edition you have an easier print menu; there you can only choose with "Imposition layout" some preferences for label print. By the X8 edition you can set the quantity of rows and columns with "Page Layout".

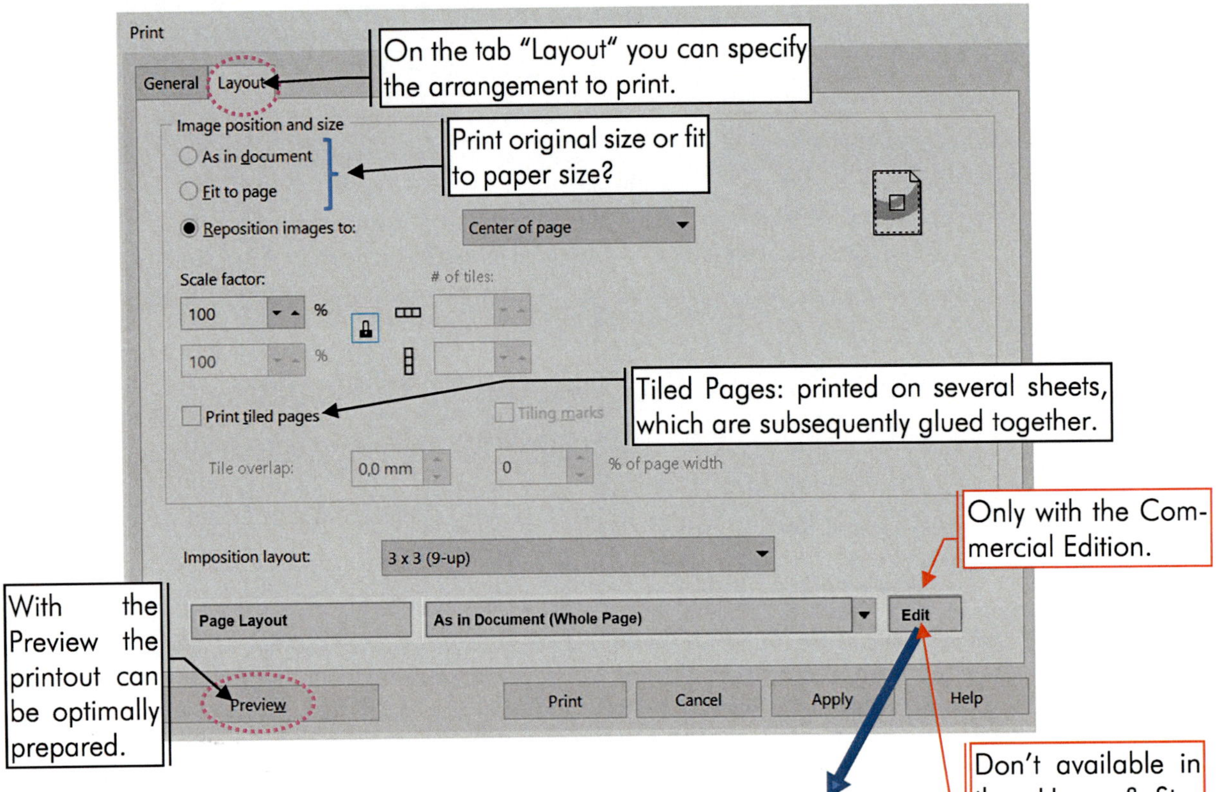

By the Commercial Edition you can choose „Edit" by Page Layout:

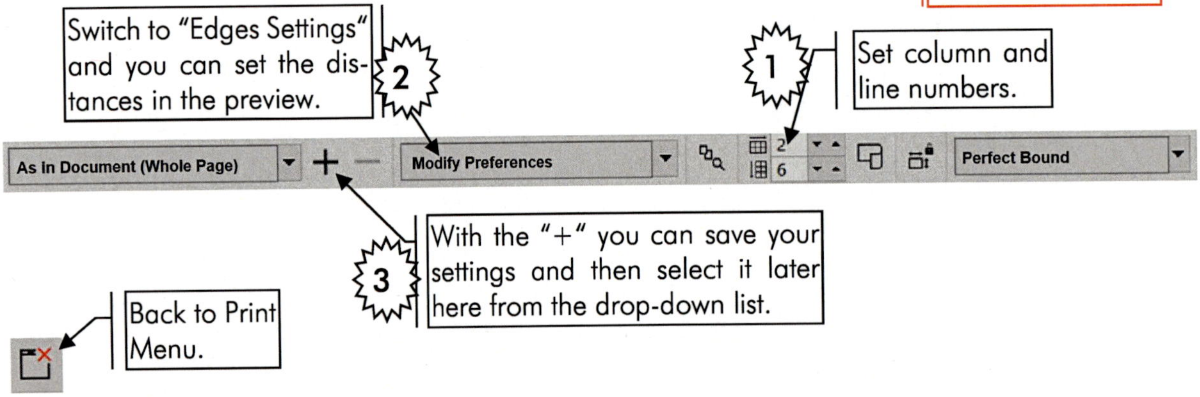

- ➢ Close this menu, switch on the Preview and it if all matches, print it out.

Another method, with a bit of manual work, but more obvious, is to specify the columns and lines with Guidelines, and to copy the first completed business card into the other cells before printing.

Chapter 20

20. Pictures and Text

You already know the word processing, including Paragraph text, the snake is already drawn and how pictures are inserted has already been explained in the exercise on page 89. Consequently, the prospectus should now be finished without any problems.

It is supposed to be a folded sheet with 5 folded columns. So that the exercise does not take too long, this is cut here on three sides. And the original images were replaced by images from CorelDRAW or from the Web.

- Open the exercise Snake from Chapter 17 and save it under the name AFS folder.
- Instead of one page, we now need to set up three, that is, page format three times as wide as 300 mm.
- You can now set the following vertical Guidelines: 10, 90/110, 190/210, 290. In the case of known coordinates, the Guideline menu is advantageous (right mouse button on the ruler, then select "Guidelines Setup").
- Mark the snake side (snake and address text) with a large marking frame (Pick Tool) and drag it to the right page.

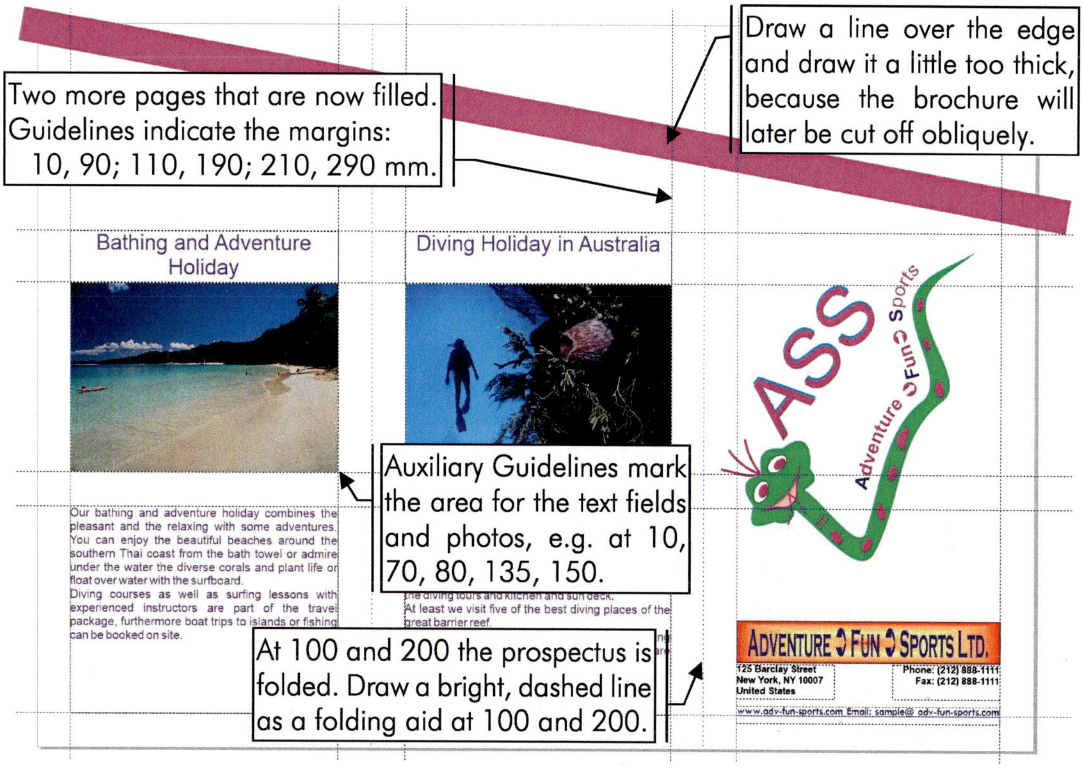

20.1 Insert Photos

Now we have three sides, two of which are still empty. Let's add the photos first. How to do this with Connect has already been described on page 89.

- Now we search for photos on the Internet: start an Internet browser and search e.g. by www.msn.com or www.google.com, matching photos for our flyer as "travel" or "beach" or "scuba" and switch to "photos".
- Open suitable photos, copy with right mouse button-copy and insert in Corel, also with right mouse button or the symbol.

  ↪ If you save the photos on your hard drive, you could insert it in CorelDRAW the folowing ways: using the symbol "Import", from Corel Connect, or open the folder in the Windows Explorer and drag into CorelDRAW.

- Adjust the size roughly and move it to the desired position with the left top handle matching to the Guidelines, then finish by moving the size to the right bottom Guideline corner.

  ↪ Change the size of images only at the corner points, otherwise the size ratio will be distorted. If this happens, immediately undo or re-import the image.

Arrangement of sample pictures:

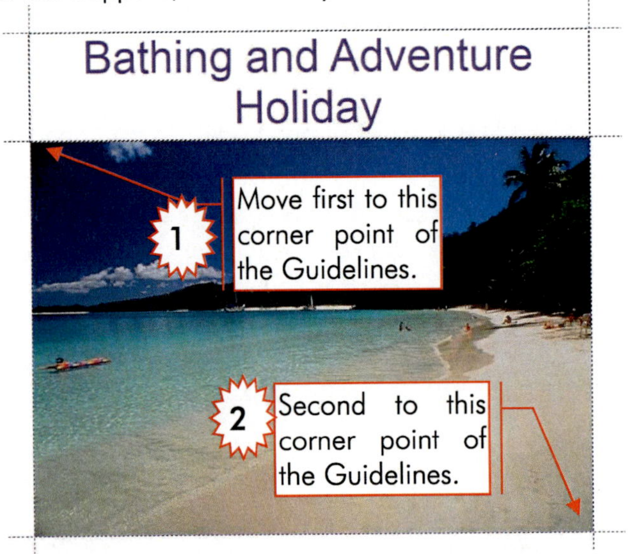

Do not look for the original example photos, but similar ones from Connect or from the Internet.

20.2 Cut Edge Areas of Photos

Most times the size ratio doesn't exactly match our photo area. Simply enlarging or compressing is sometimes possible, but sometimes the size ratio gets disturbed visibly. Then we cut the edge areas with the Shape and Crop Tool:

Use the Shape Tool to mark both edges with a frame and drag to the help line corner to cut the image.

Also possible with the Crop Tool to mark the remaining area and confirm with return.

20.3 Insert Paragraph Text

- Drag a Guideline over the first image so that all the sets of text frames can be arranged at the same height, then set them.

a Paragraph Text frame over the column, write the heading, and center it.

Paragraph Text frames can be resized or moved like rectangles at the handles.

A set of Paragraph Text frames for the description text. Set this with 12 pt and block set.

Between paragraphs, a space is positively noticeable. How this is set, you will see below.

20.4 Text Formatting and Hyphenation

You can format the Paragraph Text similar to the Graphic Text, except that all setting options for a good writing program are available for the Paragraph Text. You will find most of the settings in the Properties bar.

For further paragraph settings, use the A symbol:

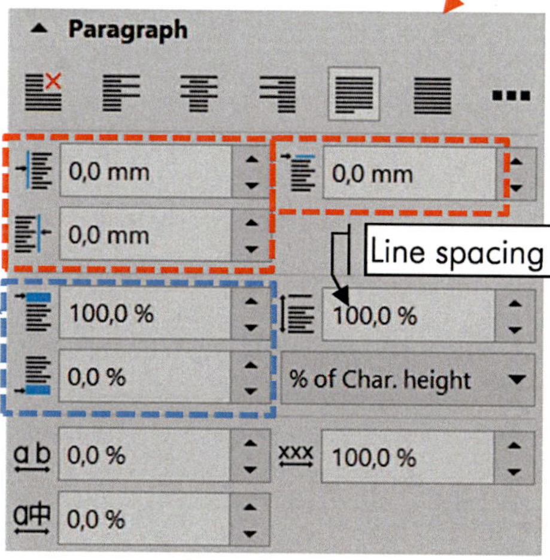

Left and right paragraph indent, and first line indent.

Line spacing

Paragraph spacing before and after the paragraph.

Hyphenation

By Text/Hyphenation Settings the hyphenation can be adjusted, with Text/Use Hyphenation you can activate it, which is particularly recommended for Paragraph Text.

20.5 ADD A PAGE

The back of the page will be filled with text and images like the first page, where we insert a normal page and print it later in two stages: first the front, turn the paper, and then the backside unless the printer can duplex.

At the bottom left you can add (empty) pages:

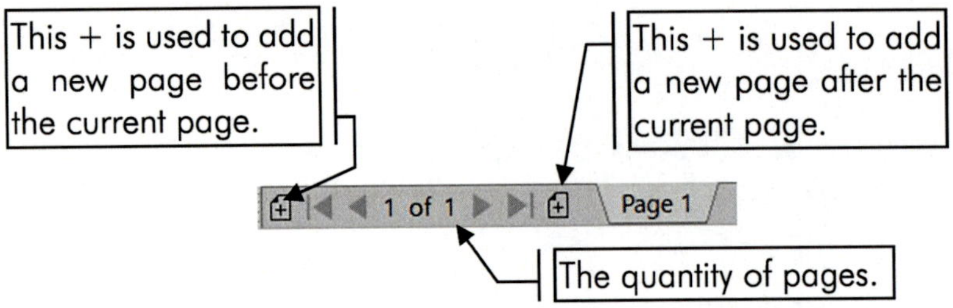

➢ Add another page. If done, you can change the pages at the bottom of the page:

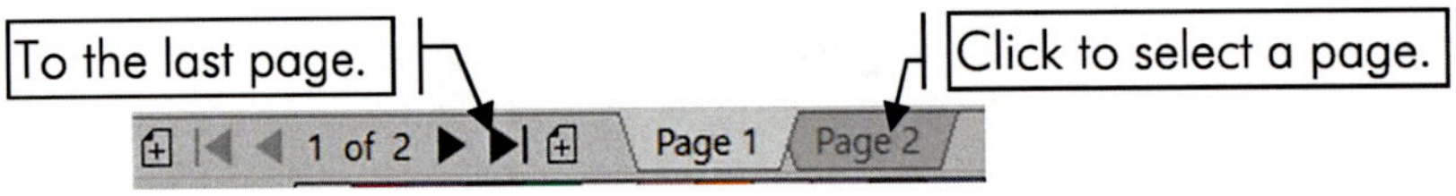

➢ Copy the top line to the back and mirror it.

➢ Add more photos from the Internet or from Connect and set in the desired positions, then add sample text as shown, matching your pictures, of course.

Find matching photos and arrange them in the columns:

The Dream of Flying

Get into the air!
Whether with the paraglider, parachute, or as a glider or parachute, a paragliding safari, with hot air balloon, bungeejumping or bodyflying.

Get out into Nature

Riding with the horse or with the engine sled in Canada, Germany, Austria, Italy, France, USA etc.
Climbing, adventure camps, spelunking (caves) etc.

Set the font size, type etc. again and again manually? First copy a selected text frame, then overwrite the text, or copy the text settings with Edit/Copy Properties From...

As in a good writing program, we can store the text settings in one style and assign them to other paragraphs as often as you want. This is presented in our progress book filled with more professional exercises.

20.6 Edit Photos

In CorelDRAW, you can cut the edges of the image with the Shape Tool, while marking two handles with a selection frame so that it is not crooked.

Photo-Paint

With Effects/Adjust you'll find the commands to change the brightness, contrast and more and with Bitmaps you'll find all effects for photos from Corel Photo-Paint. In our book about Corel PHOTO-PAINT you will find a description of these numerous effects for photos. If you press the right mouse button on a picture and select Edit bitmap, PHOTO-PAINT is started.

The important icons of the Property bar for photos:

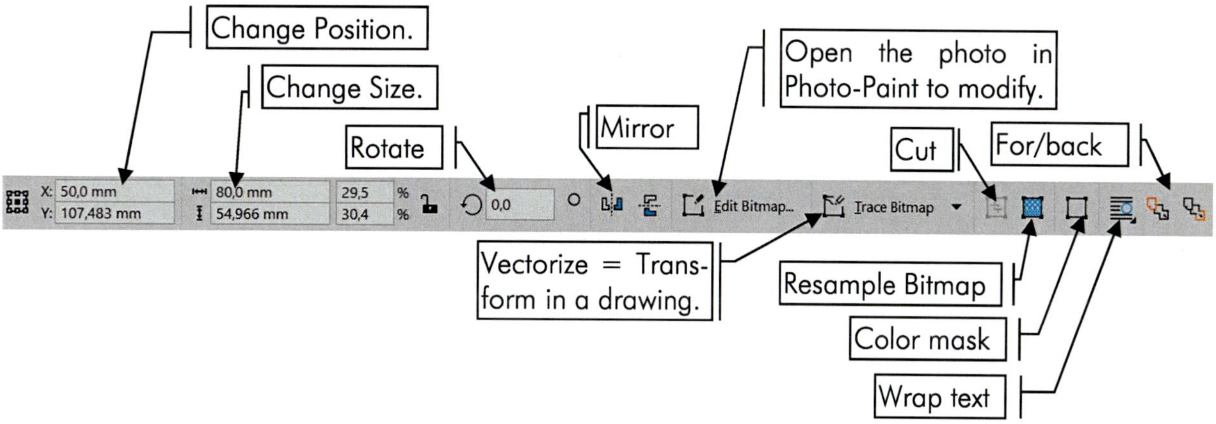

- Rotate: images can be rotated, which is also possible with the mouse as with any other element.
- Photo-Paint is the program for photos. All images (photos) in the computer are so-called pixel images. Therefore, editing is quite different from CorelDRAW, so a separate program is used. More about Corel PHOTO-PAINT in our book on this program.
- Vectorize: This allows pixel images to be converted into vector drawings, which means that photos can be converted into graphics, which usually does not yield any results that would be suitable for further processing since too many lines and turning points are created.

In the menu Bitmaps:

- Resample: a menu appears in which you can reduce the size or resolution (= number of pixels = dpi = dots per inch) of a photo, which naturally also decreases the quality (sharpness) in addition to the file size.
- Bitmap Color Mask: in the window that appears, you can use the Eyedropper Tool to pick up colors from the image to hide these colors.
  - ↳ This is convenient to hide e.g. a largely monochrome background.

Transparent

  - ↳ The reverse way that the recorded colors remain visible is also possible.
- Right mouse click/Wrap Paragraph Text: You can select whether the text is to run outside or over (= every click change) for graphic elements or photos. Over the photo e.g. to use an image as a background.

Fifth Part

Effects

for Text and Extrusion

Chapter 21

21. Effects for Text

For a better overview, we begin with the effects, which are mainly suitable for text. Further effects follow in the progress band.

> Copy each sample text a few times so you have enough material to try out!

21.1 Interactive Effects

Most of the effects can be found as interactive menus on the left in the toolbox:

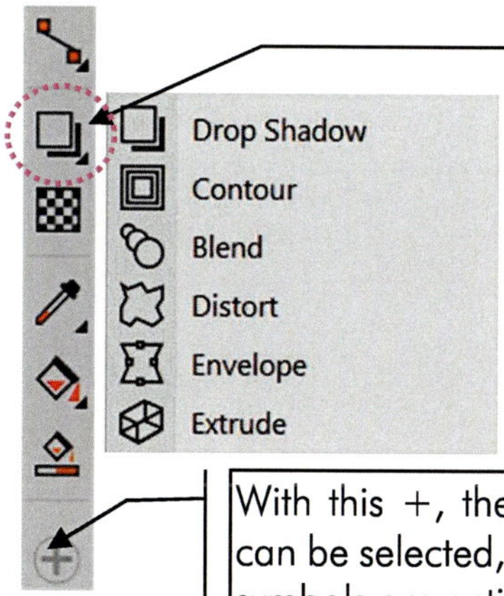

Press and hold down the left mouse button to open the selection menu: shadow, contour, blend, distort, envelope, extrude.

With this +, the displayed symbols and submenus can be selected, more precisely deselected, since all symbols are activated.

Transparency effects are not in this effects menu, you find them separate under this icon:

In these interactive menus, you can specify the settings in the property bar or by holding down the left mouse button.

The old method by means of a command for effects is however at the beginning at least more clearly, since a menu is opened, in which the setting possibilities are clearly recognizable.

Therefore, we start with the Effects menu, the interactive commands are described in the progress band, but can also be applied without guidance if the effects are known.

Examples of the interactive effects and their applications can be found in Chapter 15 on page 93.

21.2 Move Letters

The easiest effect: letters can be positioned anywhere with the left mouse button (only in graphic text).

- New graphic and write as Graphic Text: Hello! Copy it a couple times.
- Choose the Shape Tool and you can move letters at the handle points.

Use the Shape Tool to pull letters apart:

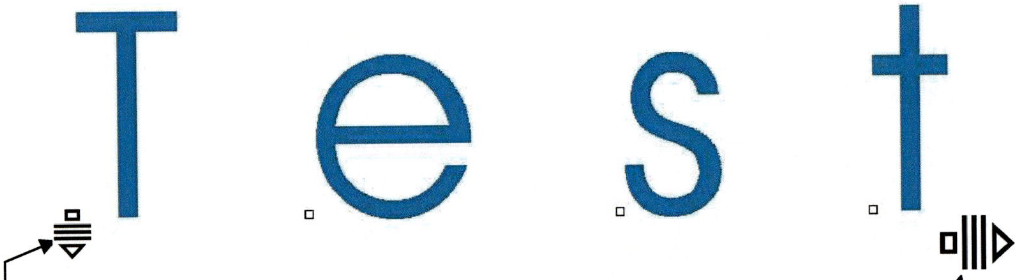

For multi-line text, you can change the line spacing here.

At this symbol, text can be stretched or compressed.

21.3 Add Perspective

- Choose another copy of the sample text.
- Start with: Effects/Add Perspective.

Corel switches to the shape tool and you can move points with the mouse the corner so that a perspective can be set.

Notice the vanishing point, which can also be moved with the mouse. The two lines of perspective converge into this vanishing point.

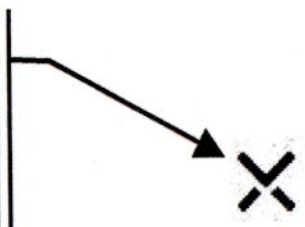

With Effects/Clear Perspective you can remove them at any time.

21.4 The Envelope Effect

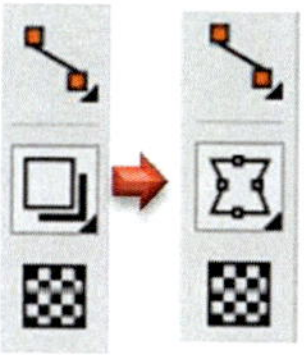

- Choose the next copy of the sample text and start with Effects/Envelope from the tool bar left side.
- Now you can modify the envelope at the handles

  ✎ NOTE: If you want a straigt envelope, you can delete the turning points in the middle.

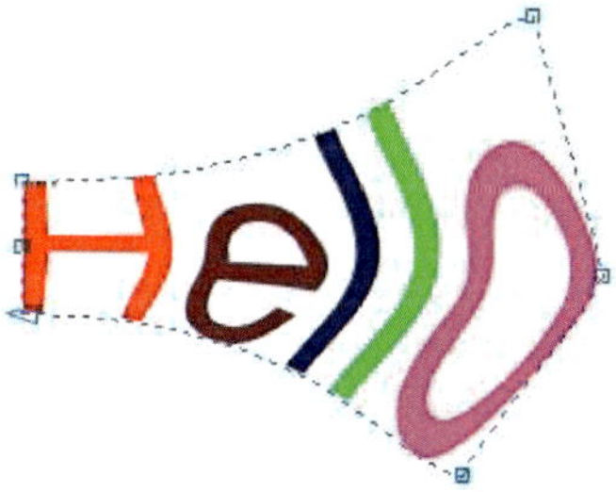

Further settings you find in the Property Bar:

A Preset, rectilinear, slant, pinch… can then be changed as desired with the Shape Tool.

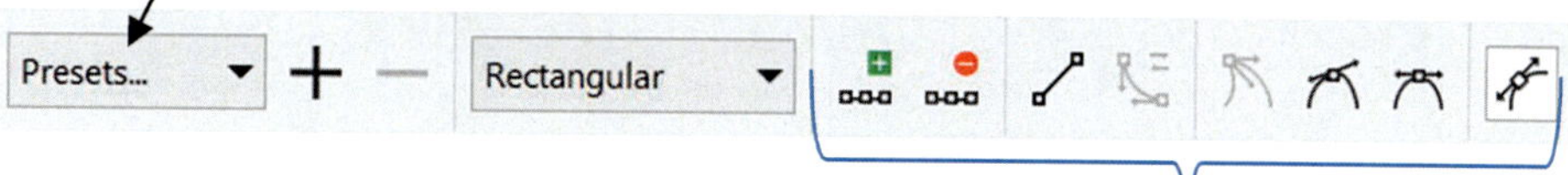

You can add or modify turning points as in the chapter about the form tool described.

Straight line or an arc line for a trumpet?

Instead Putty (elastic) you have you have this possibilities: horizontal, vertical, original, but you can't switch after drawing, you must set before you perform the envelope:

Horizontal: the text is adapted to the envelope horizontally. Mostly illegible result.	
Original: the shape is maintained half way.	
Vertical: the text is adjusted vertically to the envelope.	

21.5 CONTOUR

Here we can create different colored steps around the object or within it. The example shows this.

➢ Select a new example text, then Effects/Contour:

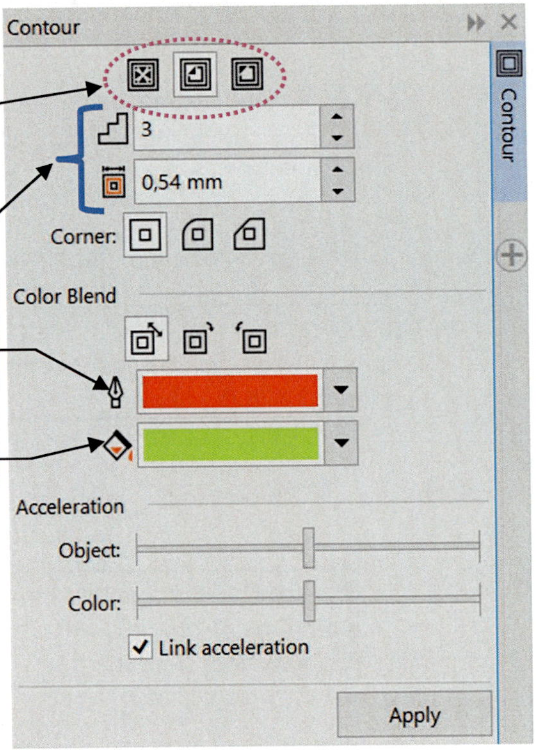

To center, inside or outside.

Steps = Number of contours (stripes).
Offset = Width of strips.

The normal fill and line color can be set with the mouse. The line color of the object changes to this color step by step.

The fill color set to the text moves each step to the color specified here.

Contour outside with red text color:

With contour inside:

- To Center: Corel automatically creates as many contours (steps) as needed to match with the specified width (Contour offset). Therefore, the number of steps cannot be selected but only the width.
- Many steps with a small distance lead to soft color traces.

➢ Start with a contour outwards to see the effect.

The Colors:

Here you can choose the way through the color disk from object color to Contour fill color:

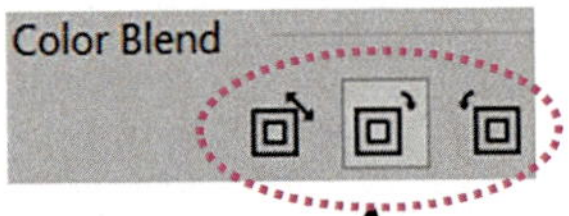

The colors of the stripes change from the filling color of the object to the fill color choosed in above contour menu, same for the line color.

Straight / clockwise / counterclockwise.

Possible Problems:

- Contours inwards do not seem to go if the distance is set too high! Even too think of a line makes the filling color unrecognizable.
  - ↳ Possibly start with a contour outwards, in order to be able to recognize the width of the strips, then try inward.
  - ↳ Increase as much as possible to see the effect, especially with a contour inward.

Chapter 22

22. Extrusion

Finally! The classic effect. We will go through all of the settings.

- Write the sample text EX and set a very large font for it.
- Copy this text several times to have some exercise material, then select a text and choose Effects/Extrude.

22.1 The Depth of the Extrusion

The setting options are divided into some menus. First the depth:

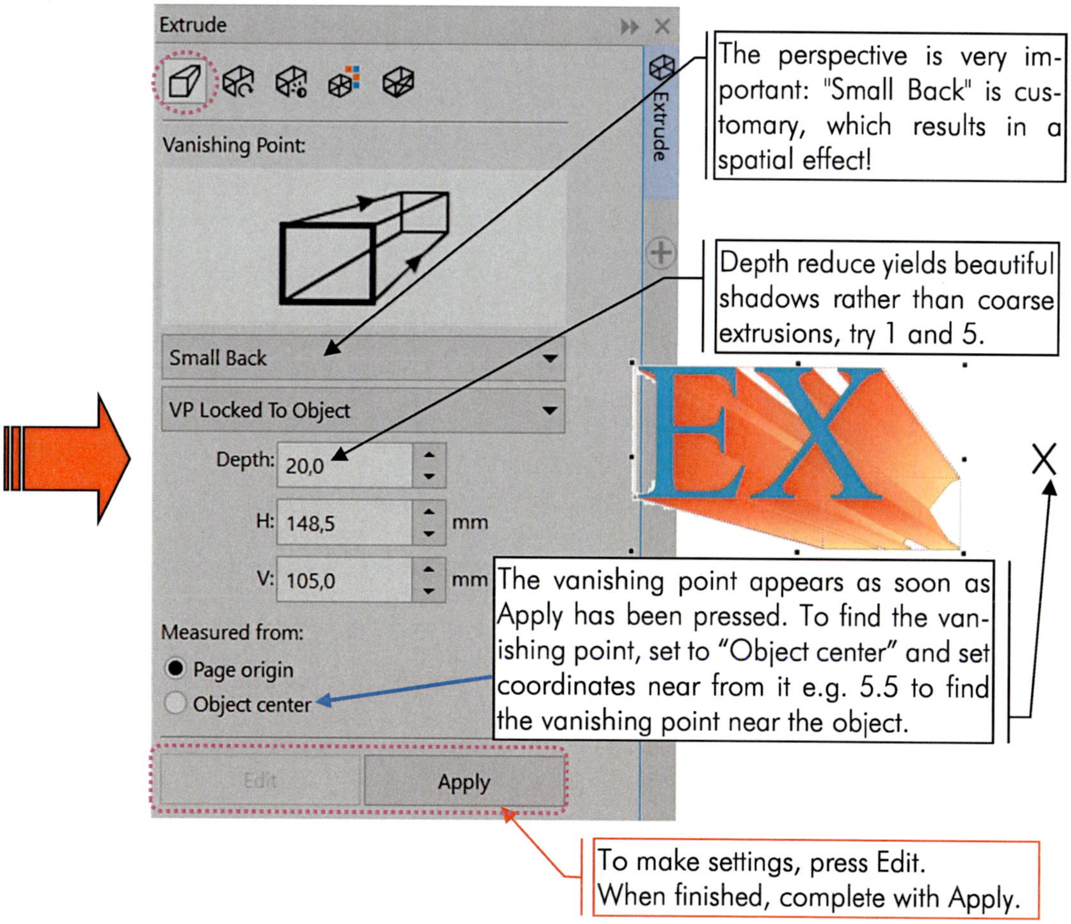

With color the extrusion is particularly beautiful - follow immediately.

22.2 THE COLOR

Extrusions are only really beautiful with colors.

➢ Choose the fill color from the color palette with the left mouse click, the line color with the right. In addition, the color for the extruded surface can be set on this card:

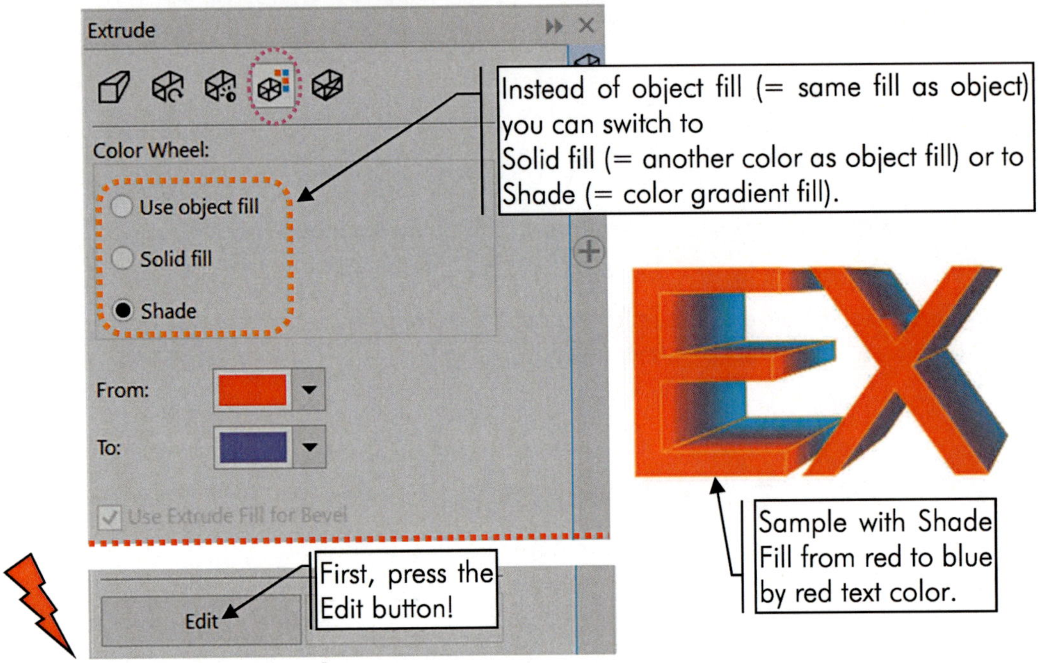

22.3 THE ROTATION

Objects can be rotated on the second card:

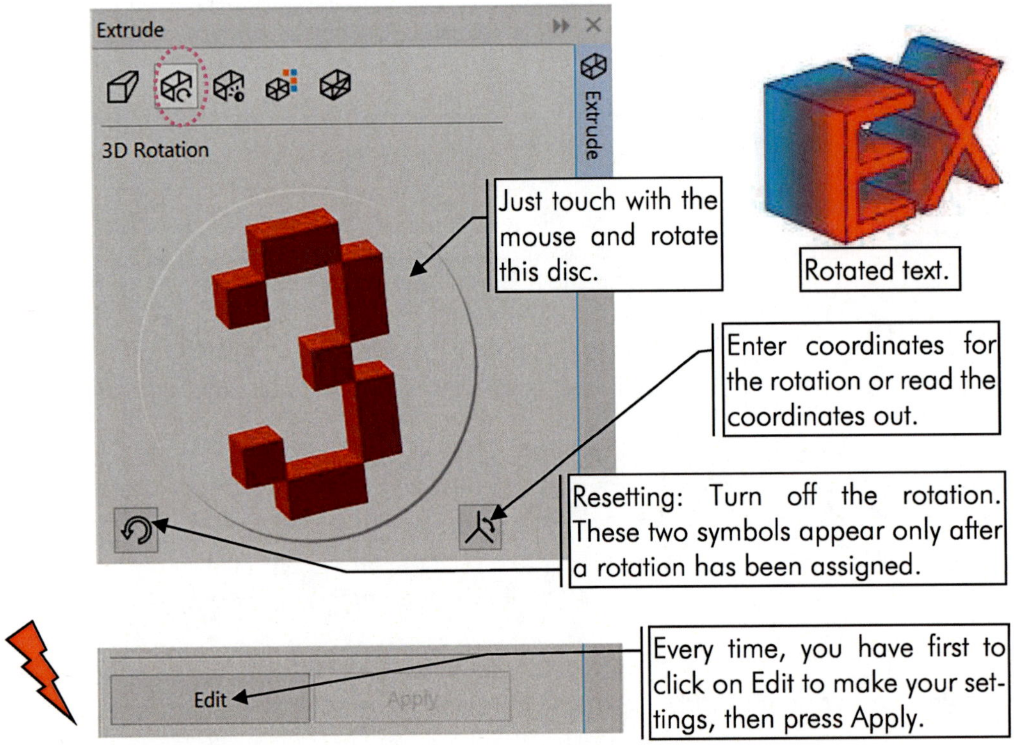

22.4 Light and Shadow

For real objects there is always light and shadow. For this, we can place up to three lamps in Corel, which not only illuminate our object, but also create the shadow pages. Each of these lamps can be regulated by their luminosity.

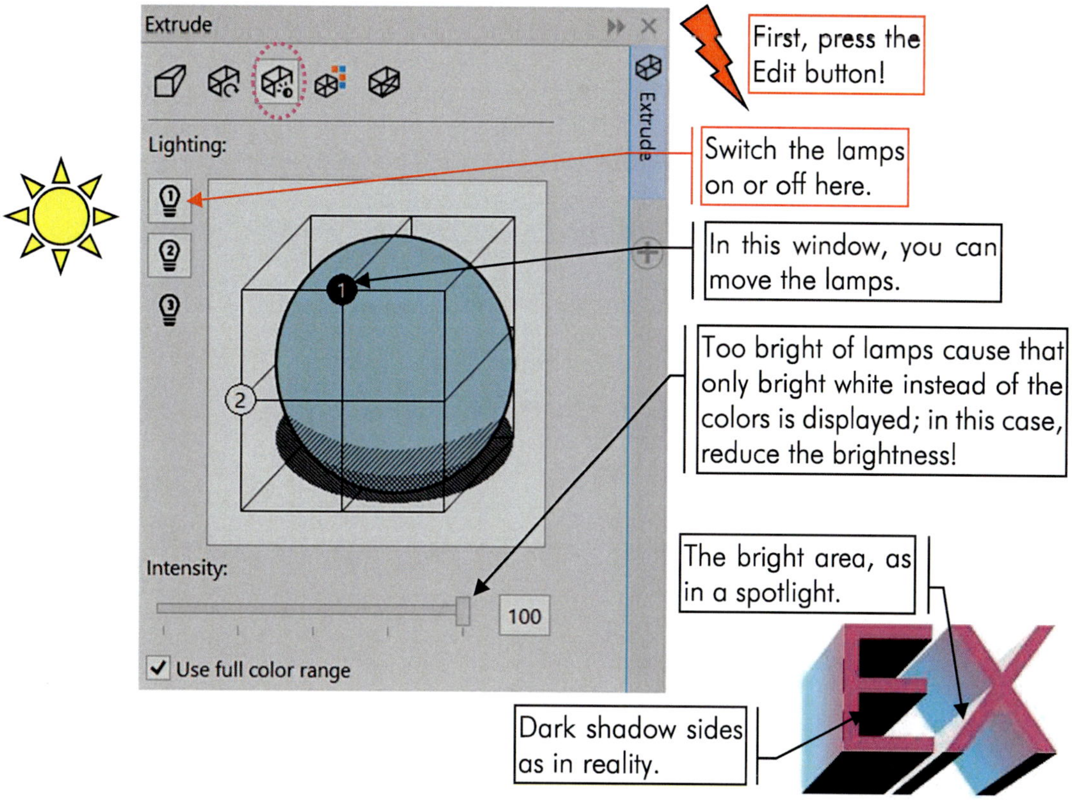

22.5 Bevels

Here sharp edges can be replaced by bevelled surfaces, which is the case with all natural objects, so that the objects become even more realistic.

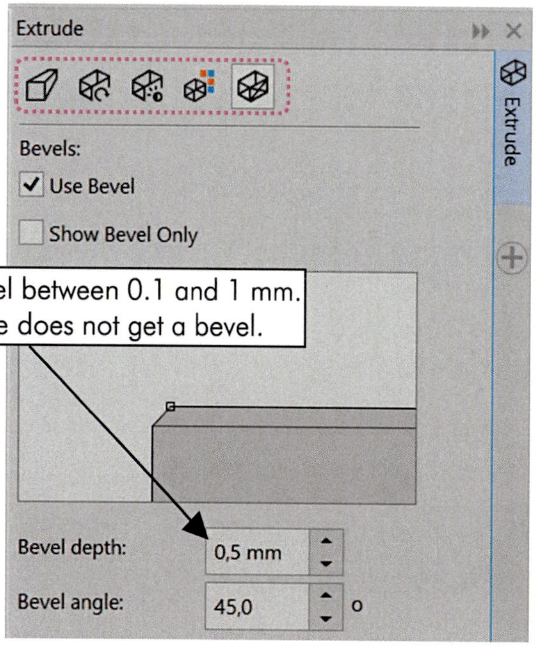

For small objects, use a small bevel between 0.1 and 1 mm. Unfortunately, the extruded surface does not get a bevel.

Don't forget Edit and Apply.

22.6 A TITLE SHEET

Last exercise, a trifle: A title page for a book.

- New drawing with size e.g. 23,5x17cm, set grid and guidelines as border lines and write each line of text separately, then align with the left and right guide lines.
- Then, extrude the first line with short depth, highlight the next line, and clone with Effects/Clone Effect/Extrude from the extrusion of the first line (you have to click then on the extruded area). By cloning, changes to the original are automatically transferred to the copies.

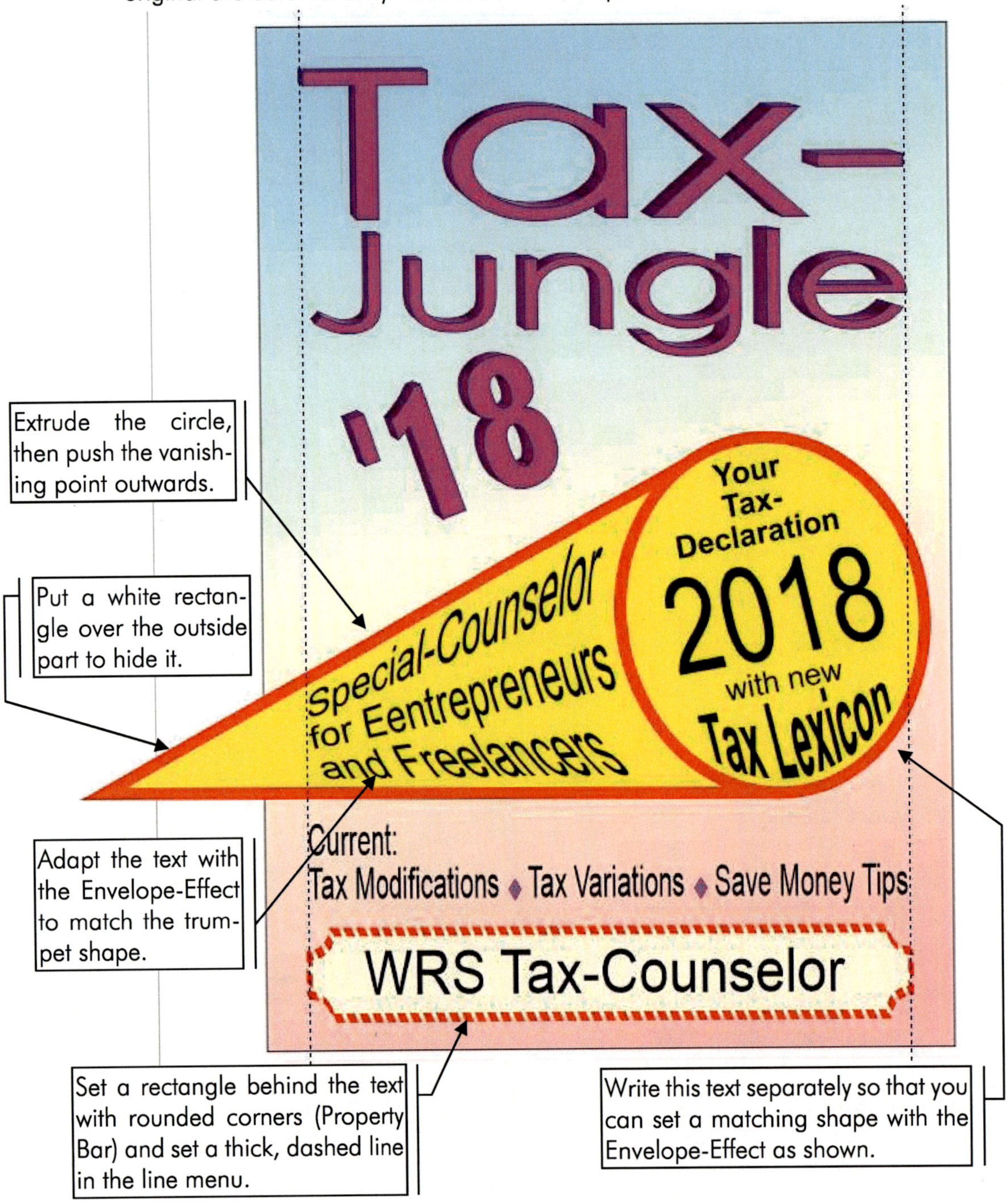

- At the end, draw a rectangle across the whole page to which a color gradient fill is assigned. Finally, place this rectangle backwards.

22.7 Exclusion Exercise: Extrusion

Try, at last, the following:

- New drawing and first set the paper format matching (how big you want to print out?), then write both text blocks separately.
- Turn them to the same angle and extrude 2018.
- If the extrusion is finished, mark the other text and Effects/Clone Effect /Extrude from, then click on the extruded area.
  - Thus, the other text has the same extrusion, possibly reducing the depth of the extrusion, since the font is smaller.
- Finally, draw a rectangle as large as the page, with a conical or radial color gradient filling and put it in the background.

Stars with the polygon drawn + Drop Shadow that was offset.

22.8 Summary Shadows

- In the above exercise, we have created a spatial shadow through an extrusion.
- Also, remember that you can create a minimally moved copy as a shadow using Object/Transformations/Position (s. S. 61).
  - Assigning a different color to this copy creates a nice shadow.
  - You can create a gradient shadow using the Drop Shadow Tool, described on page 91.
- Of course, the effect contour could also be used to create a soft-running shadow.

Notizen: ....

....

....

Chapter 23

23. Index

I

L

M

N

O

P

Q

R

S

T

U

V

W

Z

Chapter 24

24. Summary

Basics:

➲ Save cleaned up work in Folders + Subfolders and make backups!

➲ Most important programs of CorelDraw Suite:
- CorelDraw (cdr): a vector drawing program = for presentations, covers, advertisement ..., combine photos, graphics and text here.
- Photo-Paint (cpt): pixel = dots, for photos and photo editing.
- More: Font Navigator (font manager, only by X8), Capture (make photos from your monitor), Connect choose ClipArt or Corel Web Content...

Basic Structure:

➲ Commands - Symbols – Property Bar - Toolbox,

➲ Rulers - Scrollbars – Color Palette,

➲ Dockers for more functions, e.g. Transformations, Effects...

➲ [Ctrl]-z: undo,
- Delete: mark the object + [Del]-button.

To Draw:

➲ Basics: Line, rectangle, ellipse, polygon, shapes and Pick Tool.

➲ Line- and filling settings.

➲ Freehand-Lines:
- First click: start point,
- Next click: end point of a straight line,
- DoubleClick instead single click: add a line,
- With pressed mouse button freehand drawing.
- Polyline: single click for next line, double click for end point.

➲ Square + Circle with [Ctrl]-button.

Colors:

➲ Pick up a color: mark the object and click on the color of color palette:
- Left mouse button for fill color.
- Right mouse button for line color.

➲ Color Palette you can change by Window/Color Palettes.

➲ Eyedropper Tool to pick up a color from the drawing.

➲ Fill Tool for choosing and adjusting a filling.

Text:

➲ Text Tool A:
- Click and write for Graphic Text,
- Pull a frame with the Text Tool for Paragraph Text.

➲ Special Characters: Text/Insert Character or [Ctrl]-F11.

➲ The QuickCorrect replaces text automatically e.g. 1/2 to ½.

➲ Text/Align to Baseline Grid: Text around an object.

➲ Case: right mouse button over text, change case (save as new case not available in the Home & Student Edition).

Reshape and Arrange:

➲ Copy: with mouse, move object and click right mouse button on the way.

➲ Change size: click on object and then pull on the handles.
- Rotate: click second time on object and rotation arrows appear.
- Object/Transformations: Modify objects with this menu precisely regarding to size, position, mirror, rotation, etc.

➲ Object/Align and Distribute: e.g. center an object.

Set Up:

➲ Layout/Page Setup...

➲ Grid:
- Double-click on the ruler or right mouse click and Grid Setup.
- Document Grid with "Millimeters apart" and activate "Snap to grid".

➲ Guidelines:
- Pull from Ruler in the drawing or use the menu (right mouse click on ruler, then Guidelines Setup).
- If the grid is activated, the grid lines are also set accordingly.
- Delete Guidelines: click on it, then [Del]-button.
- Setup Guidelines: move with the mouse or Double-click on the Guideline: the menu appears.

Zoom:

➲ Zoom: use the Zoom-Tool, the symbols appear in the Property Bar:

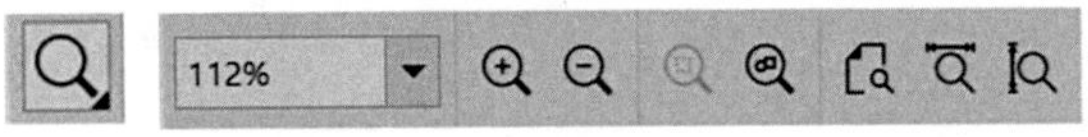

➲ or shortcuts or mouse:
- F4 or left mouse button increases,
- F3 or right mouse button decreases.

Mark:

➲ Hold [Shift] and you can mark several objects
- or pull a marking frame with Pick Tool
- or Edit/Select All... (Objects, text or guidelines)
- Note the message in the status line below! 3 Objects Selected on Layer 1

➲ To set an object forward / backward is possible with the right mouse button-Order, in the Property Bar or with the command Object/Order...

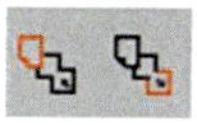

Group, Combine, Knots:

➲ Object/Group... makes a group of marked objects.

➲ Object/Combine makes possible to fill sections between the objects.

➲ Shape Tool to convert lines into Curves or to cut a circle to circular segment or to close open knots or to reshape curves.

Insert Photos:

➲ Open Windows Explorer,
- choose a folder with photos there,
- pull with the mouse into the Corel drawing,
- or insert from Corel Connect,

➲ move to desired position with the mouse and change the size accordingly,
- further you can adjust the brightness or set an effect by Effects or Bitmaps,
- with the Shape Tool you can cut borders of the photo.

➲ Export: you can save the complete drawing or selected objects into another file type:

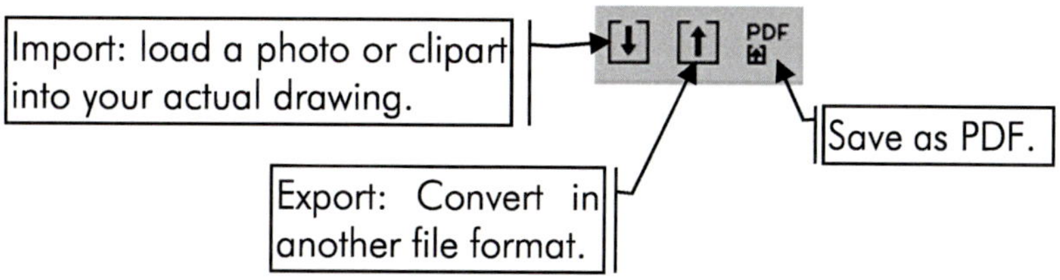

Note:

Overview Shortcuts:

[F1]	Help
[Ctrl]-z	Undo
[Ctrl]-p	Print
[Ctrl]-x	Cut
[Ctrl]-c	Copy
[Ctrl]-v	Paste

CorelDRAW-Shortcuts:

[Ctrl]-y	Align on Grid on/off
[Ctrl]-a	Select all
[Ctrl]-g	Group
[Ctrl]-u	Ungroup
[Ctrl]-L	Combine
[Ctrl]-K	Break Combination
[Shift]-[Page up/down]	Set marked object before/behind
[Ctrl]-t	Text Menu
[Ctrl]-F11	Special Characters Menu

Zoom:

[F3]	Zoom out
[F4]	Zoom marked objects
[F9]	Whole window view (back with [Esc])

Note: ....

....

....

....

....

....

....

....

....

....

....

....

....

30155336R10084

Made in the USA
San Bernardino, CA
22 March 2019